THE DECORATOR

BY

DONALD CHURCHILL

D1603036

SAMUEL FRENCH, INC.

45 WEST 25TH STREET   NEW YORK 10010
7623 SUNSET BOULEVARD HOLLYWOOD 90046
LONDON   TORONTO

IMPORTANT BILLING AND CREDIT
REQUIREMENTS

Two songs which are in the public domain appear in this play. They are "Clementine" and "Early One Morning". Samuel French, Inc. is unable to supply sheet music for these two songs. If producers do not know the tunes to these songs, other songs of a pastoral nature, such as "Greensleeves, " may be substituted.

Also, mention is made of three songs which are *not* in the public domain. Producers of this play are hereby *CAUTIONED* that permission to produce this play does *not* include rights to use these songs in production. These three songs, along with their copyright owners, are listed below. Producers should contact the copyright owners directly for rights.

"I'LL SEE YOU AGAIN"
Word & Music by Noel Coward
Warner Bros.
9000 Sunset Blvd.
Los Angeles, CA 90069

"MY BLUE HEAVEN"
Words by George Whiting
Music by Walter Donaldson
c/o Donaldson Publishing Co.
213-207-2220

"I'M SITTING ON TOP OF THE WORLD"
Music by Ray Henderson
Words by Sam M. Lewis & Joe Young
SBK Feist Catalogue
1290 Avenue of the Americas
New York, NY 10019

THE DECORATOR was first performed on October 9, 1985 at the Palace Theatre in Watford with the following cast (in order of appearance) and crew:

MARCIA_____Thelma Whiteley
WALTER_____ Christopher Benjamin
JANE _____Meg Davies

Directed by _____Leon Rubin
Designed by _____Martin Tilley
Lighting by_____ Mick Hughes

CHARACTERS

MARCIA
WALTER
JANE

PLACE

Action of the play takes place in an Edwardian mansion flat during one day in August.

ACT I

Centre is the entrance hall with front door
opening out to a corridor. Left is the living
room with a door to bedroom. Down right is a
study which is being redecorated and the
furniture is covered in dust sheets. Tins of
paint and brushes stand on some trestle
planks between two pairs of step ladders.
Upstage of this is the door to a bathroom. Enter
MARCIA in dressing gown. She looks at an
empty champagne bottle and two glasses and
enters the bathroom.
Front door opens and WALTER enters. He wears
an old jacket and shapeless jeans. He is a
battered 53.
He carries an old plastic shopping bag. He looks
round for a moment. It is obviously his first
visit.
He goes into the sitting room and tries a couple of
doors then returns to hall and opens the door to
the study.
He enters it and surveys it.

WALTER. I think I'll be happy here.

(He takes off his jacket and takes out some
overalls from his bag and puts them on. He

picks up the electric kettle and exits with it. As he crosses into the bathroom, we hear MARCIA shriek. WALTER exits fast from bathroom. Close bathroom door. During the two lines of dialogue below WALTER stares for a moment then opens the front door to check the number. He comes back in. He stands undecided.)

MARCIA. Who are you and what are you doing?

WALTER. Sorry about that, lady, but I wasn't expecting no one. (*His manner is that of the archetypal cheerful cockney.*)

MARCIA. (*Comes out of the bathroom wearing a towelling robe.*) Neither was I!

WALTER. I'm from Sykes the builders. (*Picks up kettle.*) They said the flat was empty till Monday and I had three days to do the study.

MARCIA. You've had a whole ten days to do the study!

WALTER. Not me missus. Stan was on this job but his back went out.

MARCIA. When I spoke to Mr. Sykes before my holiday in Capri he assured me that my husband's study would be redecorated by the time I returned. I got home last night and just look at it!

WALTER. Yes ... well ... it's old Stan. His back. It went again. He's got a disc on a nerve -- makes his legs play up. You do get that with Stan.

MARCIA. Why didn't Mr. Sykes put another man on the job?

WALTER. He has ... me.

MARCIA. Before today! Before today! My husband is due back tonight and will want to work in his study and it's impossible! Have you *seen* it!

WALTER. I took a cursory glance madam ... I took a cursory glance ... and without knocking Stan in any way, I reckon he must have had his twitchy legs while he was in that room..I must say ... I think you got a bit of a dog's breakfast in there.

MARCIA. And I'm not having it!

WALTER. No?

MARCIA. No, I am not having it! Mr. Sykes promised me faithfully... I told him he had ten days to finish that room and that I would be back August the 11th.

WALTER. Yes, well. You wonna have it out with him. (*She dials.*) 677-5429.

MARCIA. I know the number. Ah! I've got you at last, Mr. Sykes! This is Mrs. Hornbeam ... Yes one of your chaps has just turned up. I expected my husband's study to be finished and the flat empty. The study is half done and while I'm in my bath one of your chaps just walks in! ... No, I didn't say I'd be away till the 14th Mr. Sykes ... I said the 11th! Yesterday ... Yes I know your chap went off sick ... Yes, I've heard about his back ... Well it's very unsatisfactory, Mr. Sykes and quite frankly I'm surprised. I heard the most glowing testimonials about your firm. Good-bye. (*Hangs up.*) He might have just phoned me and let me know he was sending someone along. A little common courtesy is not much to ask surely?

WALTER. I expect he didn't phone you 'cos he didn't think anyone was here! Do you want me to split?

MARCIA. Split what?

WALTER. Go.

MARCIA. Go! No! Don't go! For God's sake! Not now you're here!

WALTER. But if you don't want me here ...

MARCIA. No! No!

WALTER. I can go and come back.

MARCIA. No! No! Now you're here -- I want you to stay and get on with the job.

WALTER. But if it doesn't suit you, madam...

MARCIA. It does! It does! I'm very *pleased* you're here.

WALTER. And so am I, madam. It gave me quite an aesthetic pleasure to get that brief glance of your body. You darting, dripping water from the bath. I was reminded of that painting by Millais of the Greek goddess coming out of a river. Diana and her bath, I believe it's called. Do you know it, madam? But perhaps you don't care for the Pre-Raphaelites?

MARCIA. I er ... I don't know it off hand. You can start then?

WALTER. I can.

MARCIA. It's your Mr. Sykes I've got a bone to pick with. I've no quarrel with *you* at all. You're just obeying orders, and for him to tell you to come along here and walk in without giving me prior notice!!!

WALTER. You'd better have it out with him, love. I'm just his floating decorator. He phoned me last night and said he had a three day job for me so here I am! That's my position, lady.

MARCIA. (*Sighs.*) Well, I suppose that in this day and age I should be grateful that I've got *someone* to carry on with the job.

WALTER. It's old Stan's back ... that's the thing. It does let him down from time to time ...

MARCIA. (*Briskly.*) I'm sure, but I'm here with just the undercoat done, all the furniture piled in the middle ...

WALTER. That's because of his back, madam. It suddenly goes galvanic and legs go jerky. As if they were electric legs. He suddenly walks .. Sort of ... (*He demonstrates.*)

MARCIA. (*Not wishing further involvement.*) Anyway ... you're here to carry on the good work ... so that's fine ...

WALTER. What he has to do is to lie on a door for a week and then he's as right as ninepence!

MARCIA. Jolly good! Excuse me. My husband's study is in here ...(*She enters the study and WALTER follows and eyes the furniture piled up in the middle.*)

MARCIA. You can carry on all right?

WALTER. Yes. I'll sort it out lady.

MARCIA. Jolly good. Mr. Sykes no doubt told you what I require?

WALTER. Two coats of mango gloss and the woodwork Trafalgar Blue.

MARCIA. Jolly good! There's a little cloakroom and loo in here ... (*She opens door.*) ... so you'll be entirely self-contained. You won't need to bother to come through the flat for anything. You can fill the kettle in there.

WALTER. Yes. That'll suit me fine, lady.

MARCIA. (*Still smiling graciously.*) Jolly good. I'll leave you to it then! (*She exits and goes into her bedroom.*)

WALTER. Jolly good.

(*WALTER takes out a cassette player and some cassettes. Selects one and puts it on. We hear Mozart's Horn Concerto.*
He lifts up the dust covers and inspects the furniture. Reads some papers on the desk. Lifts another cover and finds a phone. He goes out and knocks quietly on the open sitting room door.
Pause. He knocks again. Pause.)

WALTER. I'm expecting a business call, madam. Will it be all right if I give this number? (*Pause. He goes back into the study leaving the door open and dials the phone.*) Oh hello Dave.

Walter here. I'll be at 493-5567 till Saturday.
That's right. Cheers. (*Puts on casette.*)

(*He hangs up, covers the phone, then begins to
open a tin of paint. Door bell. Pause.
WALTER comes out into the hall. Looks at the
front door then takes a pace into the sitting
room.*)

WALTER. Your door, Madam! (*Door bell
again. WALTER removes his shoes and goes into
the sitting room. He taps on the bedroom door.
MARCIA comes out, wrapping her housecoat
round her.*)
WALTER. Someone at your front door,
duchess.
MARCIA. (*Annoyed.*) Yes. I did hear the bell.
I didn't choose to answer immediately because I
was dressing. If my front door rings again will
you just ignore it please?
WALTER. Will do, missus.
MARCIA. You just carry on with the job
you've come to do ... (*She smiles graciously.*) ...
if you'd be so kind!
WALTER. Right.. Sorry to have disturbed
you, sweetheart. (*Doorbell rings. Pause.*)
MARCIA. And please turn down that noise.

(*He exits. MARCIA glares then tidies her hair in
a mirror, then comes out into the hall and
opens the front door. JANE stands outside and*

*smiles instantly. From the hallway she can
see into the study but not WALTER. MARCIA
smiles with blank politeness.)*

JANE. Mrs. Hornbeam?
MARCIA. Yes?
JANE. Oh yes! Of course it is! Do excuse me
staring. It's just that you looked so much younger
when I saw you last night in that restaurant
holding hands with my husband!
MARCIA. (*A beat.*) I beg your pardon!
JANE. (*Sudden scream.*) You bloody whore!
(*Pause.*) May I come in?

(*WALTER has opened the paint and is about to
stir it as he overhears this.*)

MARCIA. Have we met? (*MARCIA smiles at
JANE who remains smiling and from now on the
entire interview is conducted as if both ladies
were in some kind of charm contest where the
loser was the one who got angry first ...*)
JANE. No, but I'm sure you don't want *all*
your neighbors to hear about your affair with my
husband. I wasn't being rude, Mrs. Hornbeam,
it's just that last night I really thought you were
about my age! That's why I was surprised. I was
only standing outside on the pavement, of course,
and the restaurant windows were slightly
steamed up ... so I suppose that's why I got the

impression you were nearer 30 than 50, my error. Is Brian still here, Mrs. Hornbeam?

(*WALTER moves the tin of paint nearer the door.*)

MARCIA. (*Curtly bluffing it out.*) I'm awfully sorry, but I'm afraid you're confusing me with someone else ...

JANE. Oh no, ... you *are* the lady I saw with my husband. This morning, you do look a little more mature, but you are the same woman I saw in Stefan's last night.

MARCIA. Stefan's what?

JANE. The Hungarian restaurant in Fulham. You're so *lucky*. I've often asked Brian to take me there but he's always said it's too expensive! That's married life for you! Oh no ... you really are the same lady ... if I may coin a phrase. Candlelight is so kind isn't it? But if you surprise me, Brian absolutely *astonishes* me because ...

MARCIA. Brian who?

JANE. (*Ignoring her.*) ... because he doesn't usually go for older women.

MARCIA. Really?

(*WALTER goes quietly nearer the door, to listen better.*)

JANE. (*Calls.*) Brian!

MARCIA. There is no Brian here.

JANE. As he phoned me earlier saying he was speaking from Scotland ... I assumed he was still here with you, in London. (*Pause.*) He left early did he? I wonder where he is? He can't go to his office, because he's not due back from his fishing trip till Sunday. Perhaps he's coming back here shortly?

MARCIA. (*Impatient and imperious.*) I'm awfully sorry but I haven't the slightest idea what you're talking about.

JANE. Don't interrupt me with crap, Mrs. Hornbeam.

(*Walter takes his lunch box from his bag and sits in a covered chair and has a snack.*)

MARCIA. (*As before.*) I'm sorry but I simply have no idea what you are talking about ...

JANE. Please, no bullshit. Anyway, (*Chattering on gaily.*) you can imagine my surprise when last night, as I was sitting quietly at home, my old friend Maureen rang up. "Where is Brian?" she said. "Fishing in Scotland, " I said. "Are you sure?" she said. "Yes," I said. "He phoned me ten minutes ago from Inverness." "Well," said Maureen, ... I've just seen him with a woman in Stefan's restaurant in Fulham. I know Concorde is wonderful," she said, "but surely it's not that quick?" "You saw him?" I said. "Yes," she said, "as I was passing on top of a

19 bus. The bus stopped and I got a grandstand view of Brian sitting at a table in the window and stroking some over-dressed woman." "That's not possible," I said. "I thought I must be wrong," said Maureen, "so I got off the bus to make sure! I went right up to the window," she said, "and it was definitely Brian!" Well, after she told me that, I got into my car *immediately* and I arrived in Fulham just in time to see you both finishing youʏ creme brulees ...

(*WALTER has eaten through this and reacted to everything in a manner of heightened intrigue.*)

MARCIA. I ...
JANE. Then you had a creme de menthe .. he had a brandy, then I watched you both come out, get into your car and drive off. I was poleaxed! Well, you can imagine! Fortunately, I had the presence of mind to take the registration number of your car. (*WALTER impressed.*) Then I went to the police station and I said to the nice Sergeant I'd just seen a lady drop an earring but by the time I'd picked it up, she had driven off. I gave him the registration number and waited a few moments. Then the Sergeant came back and said they would inform the owner because there were not allowed to give me information from the police computer ... (*WALTER cautions this.*) But ... I managed to peek over his shoulder as he was writing down

your name and address and here I am! Popping
round for a chat!

MARCIA. I don't know who you are or what
you're talking about. (*Pause. WALTER unable to
see what is happening puts his ear closer to the
door.*)

(*JANE whips out a mallet from her basket and
     smashes a vase.
WALTER leaps and holds his heart and kicks
     over a tin. Long pause.*)

JANE. (*Smiles kindly at MARCIA.*) Please,
Mrs. Hornbeam, no bullshit. Sorry about the vase,
but I did give you two warnings! Be fair! I did tell
you twice. It's the mallet we take with us when we
go camping. It's for knocking in the tent pegs. I
got it out of the shed this morning after Brian
phoned, still pretending he was in Scotland. I
intended to smash his head in with it, but I'll give
you some of it if you keep talking to me as if I'm
an idiot.

(*Pause. MARCIA eyes the mallet.*)

JANE. (*Amenable and chatty again.*)
Anyway, when the police contact you about the
earring, would you be very kind and say it *is*
yours, and when you collect it, send it back to me?
They're my favourite earrings you see? I'll leave
you my address ... so you'll know where to send

it. (*She puts her bag down and rummages through it.*)

MARCIA. I'm terribly sorry, I don't care if you do strike me with that mallet, I have to say I have no idea what you are talking about ...

JANE. You mean the police have been lying to me! You are not Mrs. Marcia Hornbeam of Flat 6, Waverly Mansions? And you don't own a blue Renault 5GTL registration number RTJ 679Y? The one parked outside? (*Pause.*) Anyway here's my address, Mrs. Hornbeam. (*She writes it down.*) ... for the earring. (*Puts the address in a bowl on the table.*) Recorded delivery please.

MARCIA. I'm very sorry ... I've no idea who you are! Your husband is not here! Whoever he is. *Frightfully* sorry but I just can't help you!

JANE. It's not very important. If he had been here. I would have been pleased to smash his very expensively capped teeth down his throat .. en passant .. but it's *your* husband I've actually come to see. Reginald, according to the phone book. Where can I find Reggie?

MARCIA. Not here.

JANE. I assumed that, you daft bitch, I didn't imagine he was in residence while you were here sleeping with my husband. When do you expect him back?

MARCIA. I'm not sure. He's abroad on business.

JANE. Doesn't really matter. I'll come back. I only want a quick word with him ... Just to tell him what a tart he's married to ... (*Pause. WALTER leans forward to hear better.*)

JANE. He's probably away for the same time that Brian is away?

MARCIA. I've no idea.

JANE. So as Brian has phoned me to say that he'll be arriving home this evening. I daresay your husband will be arriving home about the same time too? (*No response.*) Don't worry yourself. I'll pop back later.

MARCIA. I see.

JANE. By the way, just out of interest ... did Brian meet you the same way he meets his other ladies?

MARCIA. What other ladies?

JANE. (*Laughs.*) You didn't think you were the first did you? Goodness me no ... he's had dozens of ladies during our marriage. Mostly he meets then when I'm away at antique auctions and he's minding the shop. I don't blame him entirely, he is such a good looking swine. The last one was very stubborn. Took me ages to get rid of her, but I did finally. I managed to catch her in a pub and throw a gin and tonic in her ear. She needed seven stitches. It was still in the glass, of course.

MARCIA. I'm sorry, but I haven't the slightest idea of what you're talking about, Mrs. Erskine!

JANE. Of course not. That's why you called me Mrs. Erskine! I never told you my name, but I thought you'd blurt it out if I got you going enough!

(*She beams at MARCIA like a jolly, reassuring social worker.*) Tell you what, I'll pop back at five. You might have more news then about your husband's return. Doesn't matter if you haven't! ... I'll pop back tomorrow ... if I don't catch him then, I'll pop back again. And if I'm unlucky .. I'll keep on popping back till I am!

MARCIA. I see.

JANE. I'll let you go back to bed now. So sorry to have woken you up. It's that wicked husband of mine keeping you up all night. Is it any wonder you look the worse for wear this morning? I can quite see why you were having a nice lie in! Do forgive me for disturbing you.

MARCIA. (*Her gracious facade nearly cracks now but she recovers.*) You haven't disturbed me at all!

JANE. (*Gives her sweetest peekaboo smile.*) But I will, Marcia, I promise you! (*She puts the mallet in her basket.*) Till tea time then! (*She waggles her finger in good-bye.*)

(*MARCIA slams the door. JANE is heard giggling as she walks away. MARCIA leans heavily against the door with her eyes shut as she tries to regain her composure.*
WALTER packs up his snack and stirs paint.
After a moment she goes slowly into the sitting room. She stares ahead. Then realizes something. She goes back to the hall and into the study.)

MARCIA. (*Imperious, but her voice trembling.*) Would you mind keeping the door closed? I don't want the smell of paint permeating the *entire* flat.

WALTER. I beg your pardon, madam. (*She exits shutting his door.*)

MARCIA. (*Enters the sitting room, closes the door and stares against it ashen faced.*) Oh God ... please ... just let me die!

(*WALTER carefully opens the study door and peers out at the closed sitting room door. He pads to it and puts his ear against it. Pause. MARCIA goes weakly to the sofa and sits on it and stares. WALTER looks through the key hole.*)

MARCIA. Oh Reggie! You're going to kill me! Kill me! (*She rises and dials the phone. WALTER runs back into the study and lifts the extension.*) It's Marcia, Charlotte. Thank you for telling me to go to Stefan's restaurant... (*WALTER nods and grins with malevolent anticipation.*) because Brian's wife saw us eating there. She's just been here and smashed my best vase with a mallet ... one of a pair, and tonight she's going to tell Reggie. My whole life has been ruined because I went to Stefan's last night! ... Yes well next time you hear of a new restaurant would you mind keeping your bloody mouth shut!

(*She hangs up. WALTER hangs up. She passes a hand across her brow and sinks wearily onto the sofa.*

WALTER begins to stir the paint. He goes into the hall and examines the broken vase, speculates then looks through the key hold, then straightens and taps on the door. MARCIA leaps.)

MARCIA. God! (*She puts a hand on her heaving bosom.*

WALTER. Madam?

MARCIA. Yes? Come in! Come in, come in!

WALTER. (*Slowly opens the door and puts his head round the door, apologetically, as if he was a butler and the family had just suffered a loss. His speech also goes up a couple of social notches and gradually he becomes more and more the archetypal butler.*) Pardon me disturbing you madam, but I wondered what you wanted to do about the cloakroom door?

MARCIA. (*Stares at him blankly.*) Cloakroom door?

WALTER. Leading off from you husband's study. I know you require the skirting board and window frames in Trafalgar Blue but I wasn't sure about the cloakroom door.

MARCIA. The cloakroom door? (*She rises. She is too shocked to notice this new WALTER. He obsequiously opens the door for her. They enter the study. She stares at the cloakroom door blankly for some seconds.*)

WALTER. Yes. Would madam require it in Mango gloss to tone in with the walls? Or it can be in Trafalgar Blue, to match the skirting? I'd have to do the other door in Trafalgar Blue, as well, of course. Or not. I can do one door in Mango gloss and the other in Trafalgar Blue gloss. Or both in Mango gloss? (*Pause.*)

MARCIA. Would you mind going home?

WALTER. (*Expresses refined surprise.*) Now madam?

MARCIA. Yes please. I'll pay for a full day's work. Would you mind?

WALTER. Not at all, Mrs. Hornbeam.

MARCIA. It's nothing personal.

WALTER. No, quite. Very good, madam. (*WALTER doesn't move.*)

MARCIA. It's just that I have a slight domestic problem at the moment.

WALTER. I understand, Mrs. Hornbeam.

MARCIA. (*Sharply.*) What do you mean?

WALTER. I understand your instructions, madam. I'll pack up at once. (*He begins to brush the paint from his stirring stick.*)

MARCIA. I'm sorry to have to stop you when you're half way through. I haven't anything against your workmanship at all ... I think you're making an awfully good job of it.

WALTER. To tell you the truth, madam ... I haven't even started yet ... All I've done is take the lid off a tin of paint and stir it.

MARCIA. Anyway, please don't think I'm dissatisfied with you.

WALTER. (*Bowing.*) Very considerate of you, madam.

MARCIA. Reggie did give me very specific instructions about that door before he left, but I'm afraid they've gone clean out of my head and this room is very important to him you see, for studying his papers about his fork lift trucks. He likes to be on his own in here for two hours every evening to think, and he chose the colours for this room and drew a little chart of what he wanted for the doors but I can't remember where I put it and he'll be so cross with me when he comes home tonight if I tell you to do them in Trafalgar Blue when they should be Mango gloss and ... Oh God! (*She runs out and into the sitting room and into the bedroom as she bursts into tears. Door slams shut. Silence.*)

(*WALTER rinses his brush. Phone rings. The bedroom door opens slightly and MARCIA calls out.*)

MARCIA. (*Off.*) Mr. Decorator? Could you come here please?

WALTER. (*Immediately leaves the study and removes his shoes in the doorway to the sitting room. He opens the door and takes a pace in.*) You rang, madam?

MARCIA. Could you answer my phone please?

WALTER. Certainly madam.

MARCIA. I can't talk to anyone just now. Just say I'm not here and take a message. (*Door shuts.*)

WALTER. Yes madam. (*He picks up the phone.*) Mr. and Mrs. Hornbeam's residence. This is the decorator speaking. Oh hello Mr. Hornbeam ... You wife is not here sir. Could I take a message? ... I see sir. 9:30 this evening sir ... The reason I am here is because of staff illness. The redecorating work is not finished yet, but I am now proceeding as fast as possible sir. Oh yes sir. Your wife has returned from her holiday. Yes, I believe she had a most enjoyable time. I think she has gone shopping ... Very good sir, could you tell me what colour you would like the cloakroom door? ... Thank you sir and I hope you have a pleasant journey home sir. (*He hangs up.*)

MARCIA. (*Comes out doing up her dress. She smiles, slightly red eyed but determined to be gracious and in command.*) Do excuse my er ... I was rather upset.

WALTER. Oh please madam .. Don't mind me.

MARCIA. It's just that one or two things have been getting on top of me lately. (*Hastily corrects herself.*) I don't mean *that* of course!

WALTER. What madam?

MARCIA. (*Then brightly*.) Who was it on the phone?

WALTER. Your husband, madam. Phoning from Bahrain to say that his flight has been confirmed and he expects to arrive home around 9:30 this evening madam.

MARCIA. Oh shit. Excuse me. Thank you very much.

WALTER. He also asked me whether you had had a pleasant holiday in Capri with your friend, Charlotte.

MARCIA. (*Anxiously*.) And you said?

WALTER. I believed you had had a most enjoyable time with her.

MARCIA. Thank you.

WALTER. I then explained to him about the delay in finishing his study.

MARCIA. Was he peeved?

WALTER. He didn't appear to be, madam. I asked him about the cloakroom door and he said Mango gloss.

MARCIA. Oh good.

WALTER. I said that I would be proceeding with the work as quickly as possible and this seemed to please him.

MARCIA. It did?

WALTER. But as you would prefer me to leave, I shall put the lid back on the paint and go home and await your further instructions.

MARCIA. Thank you.

WALTER. Will that be all, madam?

MARCIA. Thank you.

WALTER. I hope you feel better soon, madam.

MARCIA. Thank you.

WALTER. I'll only be a few minutes then I'll get myself off. You want to be alone. I do understand.

MARCIA. (*She eyes him.*) No doubt you overheard every word that dreadful woman said to me?

WALTER. (*Expressionless.*) I'm sorry, madam?

MARCIA. All those terrible lies! (*Because of WALTER's apparent fatherly sympathy, her simmering hysteria now has a certain vulnerability. We feel she wants to discuss her problem with him but doesn't know how to bridge the social barrier.*)

WALTER. Well since you ask, madam, I did happen to catch a *snatch* of her conversation as I was thinning my emulsion ...

MARCIA. So sorry. Awfully embarrassing for you.

WALTER. Not at all, madam. I only hope my presence wasn't an embarrassment to you. I'll just get changed now, madam, and be off.

MARCIA. (*Abruptly.*) Would you care for a cup of coffee before you go? I'm sorry I don't know your name?

WALTER. Page, madam. Yes, I'd like a cup of coffee if you're making one ...

MARCIA. (*Strident,*) Please ... *don't* say "if your making one." If there's one thing I can't stand, it's when you offer people a cup of tea or anything and they say "yes, if you're making one"! I can't stand it! Honestly! It's one of those things that drive me raving mad! I'm getting my nervous rash now. That's all I need. It's going right across my back. (*She scratches herself.*)

WALTER. (*Pause.*) I'm sorry, madam.

MARCIA. (*A neurotic flow.*) "Yes please" or "No thank you" ... but it just gets right on my top note when people say ... "If you're making one"! My intentions are of no concern to them. I'm offering them a cup of coffee because *I want to offer them a cup of coffee!*

WALTER. (*Slight pause.*) I'm with you madam.

MARCIA. (*She scratches her thigh. Slight pause. She screeches and swats something.*) There's a fly! Don't they send you barmy! (*Pause.*) There's no flies in China, did you know that?

WALTER. (*Slight pause.*) No, that's news to me, madam.

MARCIA. Oh yes! They gave a directive saying that flies do not serve the revolution. Every time you see a fly you've go to kill it! Wonderful idea. They're doing the same with dogs now.

WALTER. (*Politely.*) They don't serve the revolution either?

MARCIA. No ... Two things I can't stand ...
Dogs and flies ... (*Slight pause.*) ... and people
who say "only if you're making one." Yes ... that
woman is quite mad, of course. But I expect you
could tell that by the tone of her voice? (*She
searches the room.*)

WALTER. Well, since you mention it
madam ... I thought I detected a note of hysteria in
her voice.

MARCIA. Oh yes! Raving mad. But you do get
that round these parts. You get the strangest people
knocking on your door. I think it's something to
do with living so close to Harrods. (*Scratches.*)
My damn itch has come back with a vengeance
now! Have you been in there lately?

WALTER. No, madam. I shop locally in
Islington for my bits and pieces.

MARCIA. (*High pitched.*) Just go in there!
Just *see* all those foreigners trying on cashmere
jumpers! It's like walking through some Kaspah!
Would you mind awfully scratching my left
shoulder blade?

WALTER. Certainly madam. (*As he
scratches it the phone rings. She jumps.*)

MARCIA. It's that dreadful mallet woman
again! Please answer it! Say you're the decorator
and you know nothing! You know nothing about
anything! Do you understand! Have you got that!

WALTER. I have madam. (*He goes slowly
and very dignified to the phone and picks it up.*)
Mr. and Mrs. Hornbeam's residence. (*A beat.*)

493-5567 (*His accent changes to the off-London we heard at opening.*) This is Walter speaking. Hold on, Dave. (*He writes on a pad.*) Twelve fifteen Monday 28b Soho Square. I will. Thanks. Cheers. (*Hangs up and resumes his role as he clears his throat.*) It was for me, madam. Hope you don't mind but I took the liberty of giving a business associate your phone number. I tried to ask your permission but ...

MARCIA. I don't mind at all! Would you like a glass of sherry?

WALTER. Er ...

MARCIA. I'm having one. (*She pours herself a large sherry.*) Would you care to join me in a glass of sherry?

WALTER. Would there be room for us both? (*Hastily.*) Oh I do beg your pardon madam! I didn't mean that! It just came out. Just my little joke. Yes madam, I'd enjoy a glass of sherry very much. (*She hands him the big one.*) Oh! Thank you ...

MARCIA. (*She pours herself another large one.*) I'm not in a frivolous mood at the moment.

WALTER. No, I'm sorry madam. It just slipped out. I didn't mean it to ... as the actress said to the bishop.

MARCIA. (*Not listening.*) Please do my back again. (*He does so.*) No, more to the right. Excellent. You tell jokes do you?

WALTER. I think humour lubricates the social wheels, don't you, madam?

MARCIA. I can't tell jokes. (*Scratches as she moves away.*) What a cow that woman is. I feel quite sorry for Brian now. Am I boring you? Just say if I am and go. Don't stand on ceremony! (*Pause.*)

WALTER. Not at all, madam. I'm enjoying my sherry very much.

MARCIA. It's the real stuff you know. It's not this foreign muck you see everywhere. I must have a Valium. Well ... Talk to me ... *For God's sake! (She searches for her bag.)* Where do you live? Oh Islington! You said. My memory is going now! That bitch is really gunning for me. Do talk to me. I don't want to think, you see? anything will do ... Do sit down. (*She takes a pill.*)

WALTER. What subject would interest you, madam?

MARCIA. Do you have a wife?

WALTER. I had.

MARCIA. Is she dead? Divorced?

WALTER. She left me, madam.

MARCIA. Why?

WALTER. She never actually said, but it's probably because I'm a nonentity.

MARCIA. Did you find someone else?

WALTER. No, not really madam. I put myself on the books of this computer dating agency, Select Dates Limited, but they couldn't match my particulars.

MARCIA. I didn't think you had a lady friend ... judging by the darn in your socks.

WALTER. Does that follow madam? My wife never even sewed a button on for me. (*He tries to cover them self-consciously.*) I've always done my own running repairs.

MARCIA. The wool doesn't match.

WALTER. But it matches my red socks.

MARCIA. I see. You darned your red socks then these brown socks got holes?

WALTER. Yes ... that's the history of that, madam. Yes ... you've got that in one.

MARCIA. (*Pause. She suddenly screeches. Pause.*) Oh god! Reggie will blow a gasket. (*Pause.*) You've just been arranging your next job of work on Monday, have you?

WALTER. My phone call, madam? Yes ... but it's only my spare time work. It won't affect this job of yours at all.

MARCIA. Who is this man who phoned you now?

WALTER. The chap who gets me interviews for my spare time work.

MARCIA. Not decorating?

WALTER. No, no.

MARCIA. My husband worships me, you see. He's seventeen years older than me and always felt a bit insecure about me. Not that I ever gave him cause before Bri ... What are these interviews for?

WALTER. In this case, madam, I have to see some advertising people who are going to make a television commercial.

MARCIA. Why do they want to see you?

WALTER. Because they are looking for a typical bank manager to advertise some new kind of razor, madam.

MARCIA. (*She scratches.*) I haven't had my nervous rash for seven years! Go on. (*A beat.*)

WALTER. I don't know any more details, madam.

MARCIA. I *see!* It's some sort of spare time hobby of yours is it? Appearing in these television commercials?

WALTER. Yes, you could say it was more of a hobby than a living. The last one was eight years ago.

MARCIA. You're not a decorator at all then?

WALTER. Oh yes, madam. I'm more a decorator than anything else. Painting houses is what pays my rent.

MARCIA. You're some kind of model?

WALTER. (*Quite hurt.*) Oh no madam! I'm an actor!

MARCIA. Oh really! (*Her tone becomes more respectful. She comes over and tops up his glass.*) Have I heard of you?

WALTER. Oh no, madam. No one's heard of me, except the Inland Revenue.

MARCIA. Have you even been on TV?

WALTER. Not for some time.

MARCIA. When was your last appearance?

WALTER. March 10th, the year before last.

MARCIA. What was that?

WALTER. You won't remember me, madam, I'm not a has been, I'm a never was.

MARCIA. Do tell me! I watch TV a lot.

WALTER. Well, I was last on television in episode three of a BBC remake of The Tale of Two Cities ...

MARCIA. Really! I saw that!

WALTER. I was a French peasant who held the wool for Madam Defarge. (*Holds up his hand.*)

MARCIA. I don't remember that bit.

WALTER. Well no ... why should you? I only had one line, and that was as someone's head was coming off, so I couldn't really expect to steal the scene.

MARCIA. And I was thinking of telling him it's all over. That's the most dreadful part! Over! This morning we said goodbye and I thought this might be forever. What's you name again? Perhaps I've heard of you.

WALTER. No, madam. No one's heard of me...

MARCIA. I might have, you don't *know!*

WALTER. It won't mean anything to you. I'm not anybody. Page.

MARCIA. Page! Yes ... Page ... what's you other name! Tell me! You never know! I have an excellent memory for names.

WALTER. Walter Page.

MARCIA. Never heard of you.

WALTER. Very few people have - even my mother. She can never remember my stage name. Who is Walter Page she always says. What's wrong with the name you were born with - Walter Jack Olivier? I changed it because comparisons are odious, but I can never get through to her.

MARCIA. So you're just er ... "resting". That's the word actors use isn't it? (*Pause.*)

WALTER. Well frankly, madam, I personally have never heard any actor use such an expression when they are ... between engagements, but I do grant you, it is a word which seems to have caught the public fancy ...

(*She glares out of the window.*)

WALTER. (*Finishes his drink.*) That was most welcome, madam. Will you let my guv'nor know when you want me back?

MARCIA. I've got to deal with this made woman first ... this awful woman who wants to tell my husband a lot of preposterous lies about me. (*She crosses over and tops up his glass.*) That suburban little bitch is determined to get her revenge. It's a problem, don't you think?

WALTER. How madam? When your husband meets her, he will see immediately that she is unbalanced and then all he has to do is get the police to deal with her ...

MARCIA. (*Daunted.*) Ah yes! Quite!

WALTER. As you are totally innocent of her allegations, you have no problem, madam.

MARCIA. Trouble is Reggie has always been a bit funny about that sort of thing. He was brought up very strictly and his father is still a lay preacher in Swansea. There's a slight danger he might think there's no smoke without fire, so I'd prefer her not to meet him in the first place ... just to be absolutely on the safe side, see what I mean?

WALTER. I'm sure you'll resolve it madam. A lady in 14th century Italy had a similar problem. She dealt with it, most adroitly according to Boccaccio.

MARCIA. Who?

WALTER. He wrote the Decameron - a most entertaining collection of stories about the ingenious ways ladies deceived their husbands.

MARCIA. (*A spark of interest.*) Oh really? (*She picks up the sherry bottle.*)

WALTER. In fact, hearing that lady on your doorstep I thought of Boccaccio's story about a husband who returns home unexpectedly and finds his wife's lover hiding in a barrel. (*Italian accent.*) "Who is this a man", he says, "and what is he a doing hiding in my barrel?" he says.

MARCIA. You sound just like an Italian.

WALTER. Yes. I've got an ear for accents. I've got a lot of natural ability, but somehow my career has not maintained its early promise.

MARCIA. I'm sorry to hear that.

WALTER. I don't know why. John Geilgud plays a lot of my parts, of course.

MARCIA. Yes. I can imagine that. What did the lady reply to her husband? (*She pours him another.*)

WALTER. Well, in those days they always burned adulterous wives so, naturally, she had to so some quick thinking. (*Then Italian accent.*) "You coming home early has spoiled zee lovely surprise I'ad planned for you ..." she said. "What surprise?" he says. "This man in zee barrel," she says ... "He wants to buy it and is inside it examining it for dee leaks." Well, the man inside it hears this of course, so he gets out and says he's very happy with it and pays the husband fifty ducats and takes it away. The husband is highly delighted because he'd been trying to sell this leaky barrel for months! Oh yes madam, if you want to know how to outwit that lady, read your Boccaccio.

MARCIA. Is it a big book?

WALTER. Three volumes.

MARCIA. Oh dear! My husband will be home at 9:30 tonight. In any case, how can this 14th Century lady help me? I don't have a lover in a barrel.

WALTER. And as you are innocent of her allegations why should you bother, madam? I should just let her meet your husband and risk a little domestic unease. He'll soon see she's off her head. (*He exits into hall, puts on his shoes, then goes into the study and begins taking off his overalls.)*

MARCIA. *(Reflects for a moment, then goes slowly out into the hall and stands in the study doorway. Obviously an agonised effort.)* Actually ... to be brutally honest ... if one is *really* dotting the i's and crossing every t, I would have to admit - and this is being absolutely candid with you ... that you could say ... being totally fair ... that there is an element of truth in her allegations.

WALTER. Ah yes. I see, madam. So you do now admit to having committed adultery with her husband. *(Does not change his polite expression.)*

MARCIA. I wouldn't put it quite like that. I have had only the merest, fleeting relationship with her husband just ten days a year for the past three or four years ... and this morning we probably said goodbye forever! But this lady with a friend in the barrel ... ?

WALTER. Forget the barrel madam. It is the *principle* of her deception which might be useful viz. the introducing of someone as someone else to a third party.

MARCIA. The barrel doesn't come into it?

WALTER. No madam. First, has the lady on your doorstep met your husband?

MARCIA. No, I only met her myself for the first time today.

WALTER. Then you simply ask a gentleman friend to turn up when Mrs. Erskine is here.

MARCIA. So you heard every word?

WALTER. (*Modestly.*) I think I probably caught the salient points, madam. When she arrives you pretend to be very anguished then your gentleman friend arrives and you greet him as your husband. "Hello Reggie", you say. He'll say "Hello ... er ..."

MARCIA. Marcia ...

WALTER. Marcia. What a charming name! The gentleman needs to do nothing more but just stand there and look serious while Mrs. Erskine tells him everything. Then she'll depart in triumph ... her mission accomplished. (*Pause.*)

MARCIA. Actually, I quite like it!

WALTER. Oh it's a good wheeze, madam. That' s why it's lasted since the 14th Century.

MARCIA. But the few gentlemen I *do* know are mostly friends of Reggie's, and I'd have to tell them about my situation. I wouldn't care for that.

WALTER. Boccaccio's ladies were always getting their brothers to defend their honour.

MARCIA. My brother is sailing his boat in the Pacific.

WALTER. (*Stuffs his overalls in his bag.*) Well, in that case, madam, you've had your chips. I do hope it is not too unpleasant for you. (*He comes out into the hall.*) All the best madam. (*He puts on his crash helmet.*)

MARCIA. I don't suppose *you'd* like to be my husband for a couple of hours?

(*WALTER's hand is now on the door. It remains there.*) *classic gag*

MARCIA. I just thought as you're going to pretend to be a bank manager on Monday you might like to pretend to be the chairman of a public company this evening? It might be jolly good practice!

WALTER. I must be frank, madam, it did occur to me that it would be a role I could play with a certain panache, but it would have been very unprofessional of me to suggest myself. But since *you* have suggested ... offered me the role ... er would er? ... would there be a fee involved, madam? I have to ask this because I do have my professional status to consider.

MARCIA. Yes, of course! How much would you charge?

WALTER. Well, I'd have to go home and put on my best suit. The engagement would involve use of my wardrobe.

MARCIA. No, you're about Reggie's size. Try one of his suits. They're Saville Row and I'm sure Mrs. Erskine would know the difference between your suit and ... not that I wish to be rude about your suit, Mr. Page.

WALTER. No, I agree with you, madam. If my suit looked as good as your husband's, Saville Row would not exist.

MARCIA. What about £200 as a fee?

WALTER. Gracious me no madam! You could get Peter Ustinov for that!

MARCIA. But she might recognise *him!*

WALTER. I was thinking more of er £50 ... in cash, if that would suit?

MARCIA. What about fifty now and fifty if she leaves convinced she's been talking to my husband?

WALTER. (*He removes his helmet. Regards her.*) My word! I've never been offered a bonus for convincing an audience! That is unique! Well, yes, madam, on those terms, I'd most certainly like to accept and in view of the incentive payment, I'll wear my hairpiece for no extra charge.

MARCIA. Your what?

WALTER. I have an excellent toupee in my make-up box. I carry it everywhere just in case of a snap audition.

MARCIA. Oh no! Just stay as you are! Reggie is balder than you anyway. (*Then doubtfully.*) My husband is rather an authoritative man. Have you acted a business tycoon before?

WALTER. I've played an authoritative station master.

MARCIA. What was that in?

WALTER. I had a small part in Madam Bovary.

MARCIA. So you'd know how to act the part of a man used to giving orders?

WALTER. Oh yes, madam. You should hear my Othello speech that I do for auditions. It's got me quite a few engagements. I once got a summer season at Colwyn Bay out of my Othello. I played the lead in "Bed, Board and Romance", "My Wife's Lodger" ...

MARCIA. So you've a lot of experience behind you?

WALTER. Twelve years of it. I worked for the Gas Board till I was 38, but when my wife ran off with my best friend's wife I thought I might as well do now what *I've* always wanted to do.

MARCIA. (*Getting doubtful.*) I see.

WALTER. I'm quite fresh in the game really, so I'm not as bitter and disappointed as most actors are who find themselves totally unknown at my age. I know I'm good you see.

MARCIA. (*Very doubtful.*) I'm sure.

WALTER. It's just waiting for the lucky break. It wouldn't put me off if it never comes because I like doing it ... and that's the secret of a happy life isn't it? Doing what you like doing. That's my idea of success. I'll give you value for money, madam. I am quite good at posh parts even though I say it is shouldn't ... You mentioned authority, OK so you want authority? An authoritative husband. Let me think. Ah yes. I'll do a bit of that. (*He suddenly throws up his arms and roars ...*) Haaaaaaaaang ...

(*She leaps.*)

WALTER. Out your banners on the outside walls! The cry is still ... I will! (*Pause. She scratches herself. He resumes his normal self-effacing manner.*) Or perhaps you'd prefer an authoritative, poetical husband? (*He puts his arms out in a balletic pose. His voice is quieter but exactly same. She stares at him warily.*) I know a bank where the wild thyme blows ... (*Resumes his normal demeanour.*) A romantic husband? (*He takes her hand and kneels.*) It was no nightingale my love. It was the lark of the herald of the morn. Jocund day stands tip toe on the misty mountain tops. Rather I be gone and live or stay and die? (*Slight pause. He releases her abruptly and stands.*) Welsh? (*He goes into a terrible Welsh accent, with a mad look in his eyes.*) In the bible black night I sailed down Cydomkin Drive and even the cat was asleep. (*He resumes his normal posture.*) A Scottish husband? (*He does an equally exaggerated Scottish accent.*) Ooh! Get away with you, Dr. Cameron!

(*She gives a smothered hoot.*)

WALTER. (*He calmly puts on his crash helmet, goes out into the study and collects his bag. Comes back into the hall.*) You'll let the guv'nor know when you want me again, madam? (*He is back to his off-London accent as at the opening.*)

MARCIA. You're not going?

WALTER. I think you'd be better off getting one of your gentleman friends to help you. Someone of your own type perhaps.

MARCIA. (*Runs out to the hall as he goes to exit ...*) No please ... don't go! I need you! I didn't mean to laugh. I was just so astonished. It was just nerves! I do think you're awfully good and I'm delighted you've offered to help me. I really am in a terrible jam and I don't know what I'll do without you ... I am so sorry to have offended you! It's my nerves. They're torn to shreds. It's only ten thirty and I've had a dreadful day so far! Please forgive me...!

WALTER. (*Regards her and after a moment he whips off his crash helmet and smashes the other matching vase.*) I'm sorry. I didn't mean to do that.

MARCIA. It's unimportant.

WALTER. (*He looks at her a moment then speaks with suppressed emotion.*) I never wanted to spend nineteen years with the Gas Board, but on my demob leave from my National Service I got Betty pregnant. And my Dad, who was a gas fitter, said he could pull some strings to get me into the wages department of the North Thames gas at Cowley. I could always do acting as a hobby. I owed it to Betty to marry her. So I did. I didn't do my audition for the drama school ... I went into the wages department of the Gas Board. I was never very good at it because I didn't like doing it.

I always wanted to be an actor you see, but then we had another baby ... Twenty years later, the kids leave home and my wife leaves six months later ... I'd done my bit. I'd kept us all going for years ... it was time I did what I wanted. So I became an actor ... One day I might make it ... Meantime, I'm very happy to jog along ... waiting for the perfect part ... I love being an actor ... It's very precious to me. I don't care what I do as a decorator. I don't mind when the customers treat me like dirt ... Last week, I had to paint the same bedroom wall twelve times! Twelves times before the lady was satisfied. I didn't care though. She ridiculed me ... criticised my work ... it all went off me like water off a duck's back ... 'cos this decorating is just my rent money! It's not the real me! The real me is pretending to be someone else, and I can't allow that to be ridiculed! You can trample all over me when I come here as a painter ... but not as an actor. This is me! This is my life! This is what I've waited thirty-eight years to do! You can't laugh at my thirty-eight years, madam.

MARCIA. I do *deeply* apologise. (*Pause.*) Please do try on one of Reggie's suits, Mr. Page. (*She goes into the sitting room.*)

WALTER. (*He hesitates then follows.*) No.

MARCIA. No?

WALTER. I'm sorry. You've upset me. I don't stand here as a decorator anymore, I stand here as an actor and you've humiliated me as a professional man.

MARCIA. I am really sorry. I'm sure you'll be terribly good as Reggie! I've got every confidence in you. I do think you're terribly good. (*Pause.*)

WALTER. Show me your knickers and sing The Bluebells of Scotland.

MARCIA. Pardon?

WALTER. Show me your knickers while you sing The Bluebells of Scotland. (*Slight pause.*) That will make amends.

MARCIA. I'm sorry, Mr. Page, but I'm not quite with you. (*She scratches herself.*)

WALTER. You don't seem to understand my position.

MARCIA. (*Desperate.*) I'm not sure, Mr. Page ... obviously I've hit you on a raw spot ... I didn't mean to. Please forgive me. Do tell me your position, Mr. Page.

WALTER. I do not ask you to show me your knickers because I have designs on your person. (*Slight pause.*)

MARCIA. No.

WALTER. You are not the sort of woman I fancy.

MARCIA. No ... no, I'm sure you don't.

WALTER. Women with that upper class voice ... that cut glass accent ... those Sloane Street feet, they never turn me on.

MARCIA. No ... I do see,

WALTER. It's not that I'm indifferent to them ...

MARCIA. No.

WALTER. I positively hate them!

MARCIA. Quite.

WALTER. Women who speak with that frightfully, frightfully voice which wreaks of pampered privilege have never aroused me sexually.

MARCIA. We seem to be at cross purposes, Mr. Page. I have no personal interest in *you*. I haven't the slightest desire to arouse your interest in me. Surely we are just simply discussing a business arrangement.?

WALTER. As a woman you do not fascinate me at all!

MARCIA. Quite. I don't mind a bit.

WALTER. I'm not being personal

MARCIA. Of course not.

WALTER. And I'm not a vindictive man. Normally, I wouldn't dream of humiliating you.

MARCIA. No.

WALTER. Well that's my position. (*Pause.*)

MARCIA. Quite. (*A beat.*) Yes. (*Pause.*) ... er what is your position?

WALTER. You've got to be humiliated too, madam. That's my position. I'm not selling my professional dignity for fifty quid down and a fifty quid bonus. I'm now an actor as far as you're concerned. I'm not rubbish. (*Then pleasantly.*) But you don't have to sing or do anything.

MARCIA. (*Delighted.*) Really? Oh thank you. That's most awfully kind of you ...

WALTER. I won't ask you again.

MARCIA. I'm so very grateful. You're such a nice man.

WALTER. So cheerio Mrs. Hornbeam. I'll tell the guv'nor you'll ring him some time.

MARCIA. Mr. Page! Please ... (*He goes to the door.*) Don't go! My God ... look ... though I can't do what you ask ... naturally not ... couldn't possibly ... I'm not a stripper ... I *can't* do it ... totally out of the question, but I will increase your fee to two hundred pounds.

(*He goes out into the hall and puts on his helmet.*)

MARCIA. Very well. I need you at this point more than you need me so I'll make you a final offer of three hundred pounds. (*She goes out into the hall as he opens the front door.*) Four hundred pounds? (*He exits.*) Five hundred pounds and that is my very last work, Mr. Page.

(*He shuts the door and is gone. She stares and opens the door ... and calls down the corridor.*)

MARCIA. Mr. Page? (*A beat.*) One moment please. (*She waits. He returns to the door. She goes into the sitting room. He shuts the front door and follows her. Waits. She goes and looks out of the window. He stretches his mouth. He turns to exit.*

She quickly lifts her skirt and about six inches. He stops.)

MARCIA. (*Sings.*) Bobby Shaftoe's gone to sea. Silver buckles on his knee. (*She drops her skirt. Pause.*)

WALTER. I feel sorry for you really. It's not just that you've insulted me as an actor. No, I have to admit that an element of the class war has crept into this as well.

MARCIA. What class war?

WALTER. That's a pity because it's not your fault you are as you are ... but then I can't help being as I am either. When I did my National Service I should have been an officer. I came top of the initiative test, third in the rank aptitude test but they wouldn't take me because I didn't have a public school accent.

MARCIA. How ghastly for you.

WALTER. And the class war is the one war the British do not fight honourably. One war in which they never take prisoners. Such a pity. It's ruined our country I reckon.

MARCIA. So you are quite happy now to accept my increased offer?

WALTER. Oh no madam ... I've agreed terms, £50 down and £50 if I convince. I don't want more money. I 'm not asking you to do anything you'd find impossible like shopping at the Co-op. I wish to ridicule you as you ridiculed me. When that is accomplished we can proceed further. Where were we?

(*She pulls her skirt up to the top of her thighs.
Pause. She pulls her skirt up round her waist.
Pause.*)

WALTER. Where's the Bluebells of
Scotland?
MARCIA. I'm not absolutely au fait with the
song; you might have to help me, Mr. Page.
(*Sings.*) Oh where tell me where ... has my
Highland Laddie gone? Oh where ... (*Falters.*) ...
tell me where has my Highland Laddie gone?
(*Pause. WALTER joins in.*) He's gone to Bonnie
Scotland where noble deed are done ...
(*Scratches.*) ... and it's oh ... in my heart ... I
wish my laddie well ... (*Slight pause.*)

(*He slowly removes his helmet and walks slowly
round her. Pause.*)

WALTER. Don't call us, we'll call you. (*She
drops her skirt.*) Very good, very good. I enjoyed
that; thank you (*Chuckles.*) You husband's suits
...? I look rather good in a chalk stripe. I had a
chalk stripe when I played the Noel Coward part
in *PRIVATE LIVES* ... the Darlington Echo gave
me a very good write up. They said I was more
Noel Coward than Noel Coward ...
MARCIA. (*Nervously affable.*) Yes ... I can
just see you as Noel Coward, Mr. Page ... This is

my husband's wardrobe, in the bedroom here. (*She opens the door but hesitates.*)

WALTER. After you, madam.

MARCIA. (*As she goes into the bedroom.*) He does have a chalk stripe. (*He follows her in. Door shuts.*)

CURTAIN

ACT II

WALTER. Why did I marry you? The curse of marriage, I will chop you into bits. You are as false as hell. Away, away, away!

MARCIA stares anxiously at WALTER who stands behind the sofa in a tight business suit.
The sofa and the two easy chairs no longer have cushions and the seats are now just rubber straps making them look like pieces of bizarre modern furniture.
Upstage, on a cardboard box is a column of the cushions draped with a cloth and topped with the bust of the Victorian General we saw earlier on the sideboard. The column is about five feet high. WALTER is pointing a warning finger at the column.

WALTER. (*In ringing tones.*) Be sure of your facts, madam! (*He comes in front of the sofa with his eyes still on the column and we now see that his suit is also slightly short in the trousers. He wags his finger in front of the bust.*) Prove my wife is a whore! Give me the ... (*He gestures sweepingly into the air.*) ... ocular proof, Mrs. Erskine ... or thou hadst better been born a dog ...

MARCIA. (*Nervously respectful.*) Excuse me interrupting again Mr. Page ... (*He stops ...*

frozen in mid gesture.) ... but will Mrs. Erskine understand "Ocular proof"? (*WALTER turns from her and rolls his eyes* ...) I'm not sure I do.

WALTER. Madam ... The lady's arrival is imminent! It is now ten to five! This is not the moment to stop our final rehearsal and query Shakespeare's text! (*Walks away muttering.*)

MARCIA. (*Hastily.*) Oh I'm not, Mr. Page. I think Shakespeare's wonderful, it's just that I wasn't sure what "ocular proof" was and perhaps she won't either.

WALTER. (*Patiently.*) I'm simply asking her where she saw you with her husband.

MARCIA. (*Very tentative.*) Couldn't you just say that Mr. Page? Don't you think it might be quicker if we just used normal every day language?

WALTER. I'm speaking to her in the normal, every day language that a man would use when addressing his wife's accuser. I am borrowing from Othello, yes, but I am trying, despite interruptions, to convey his emotions in the modern vernacular. (*He sighs loudly and eases his finger in his collar.*)

MARCIA. (*Craven.*) And you are doing it *awfully* well, Mr. Page, it's just that there seems ... so much of it. And did you say, that if I got a gentleman friend to be my husband he need only say a few words ...

WALTER. That was before you asked *me* to play the part, madam! (*He stands in a Macready-*

like heroic pose, with one hand on his breast.) You have asked *me* to play the role of your wronged husband, madam, and this is the only way *I* can do it ... viz, according to the dictates of my artistic conscience! (*He shoots his cuffs - a large dismissive gesture.*)

MARCIA. But Mrs. Erskine doesn't seem to have got a word in edgeways so far.

WALTER. As far as I'm concerned the good lady ... (*Indicating the bust.*) ... has told me everything! She's never stopped talking for the past ten minutes! (*He stretches his mouth.*)

MARCIA. Really? I didn't get that.

WALTER. (*Closes his eyes patiently.*) Why would I be asking her for proof that you are a whore if she hasn't already made the allegation?

MARCIA. (*A beat.*) When did she do that?

WALTER. (*Slowly.*) I have imagined her replies during my pauses. (*He eases his tight armpit.*)

MARCIA. (*Doubtfully.*) But you haven't paused very much in the last hour, Mr. Page.

WALTER. (*A loud aside.*) Oh God ... save me from amateurs! I was *deliberately* not giving Mrs. Erskine sufficient time to reply.

MARCIA. (*Slight pause.*) I'm sorry to be slow, but what is the point of not giving her time to speak?

WALTER. Because she is not *here* You daft cow!

MARCIA. (*Frigid.*) I see! Yes, I'm with you now, Mr. Page. I just thought she was going to sit there while you went on about ocular proof and being thrown in a tank of frogs ...

WALTER. A cistern full of toads. (*Rolls his eyes.*) When the lady arrives, I shall allow her to say everything she has come to say and then adjust my improvised performance accordingly. (*He pulls down the crotch of his tight trousers.*)

MARCIA. I see.

WALTER. What I have been doing the *entire afternoon* is to imagine her last line and then I have replied! Wasn't that abundantly self evident? Obviously not. My entire performance has obviously been totally incomprehensible to you! This is even worse than when I played in Waiting for Godot in Baghdad for the British Council.

MARCIA. I'm so sorry. Do forgive me. I just wasn't very sure what was happening you see?

WALTER. Why do you think I've been pointing at that pile of seat cushions every time I finish speaking?

MARCIA. That's what first started to confuse me.

WALTER. I did that ... (*He points sharply at the cushions.*) ... to indicate that *she* was speaking! You must have thought I was raving mad!

MARCIA. Well I er ... No! No! I'm in the picture now, Mr. Page.

WALTER. You must have thought I was completely round the bend!

MARCIA. It's just that I'm a bit slow on the uptake today, Mr. Page.

WALTER. (*He glares at her for a moment, then turns away.*) Obviously we cannot rehearse the scene with any *great* precision because we lack the leading lady. All we can do is sketch out the emotional progression of my character according to the statements we *imagine* that lady will make.

MARCIA. Yes, I really am with you now, Mr. Page.

WALTER. I am a professional, madam. You are now in the hands of a pro!

MARCIA. (*Nervously sycophantic.*) And you're doing it awfully well.

WALTER. I have given my Othello many times at auditions ... I have a great affinity with him. I do know what a man feels when he is told his wife is a whore!

MARCIA. And you're doing it awfully well ... I just wondered if we need to stick quite so close to Othello?

WALTER. But how can we do any better? How can we do better than borrow from that masterpiece of jealousy and revenge?

MARCIA. No, it's all wonderful Mr. Page, but perhaps we didn't have to use *every* bit? After all ... (*Laughs nervously.*) ... Othello strangles his wife at the end doesn't he?

WALTER. And we are substituting the slap, madam. This is what we've been rehearsing ...

MARCIA. That's another thing. Do you *have* to slap me?

WALTER. I'm sorry, madam ... but if I do not suit you, if you don't like what I am doing I shall be *very* happy to get out of this tight costume and go home! I've got my fifty quid, I can happily go home!

MARCIA. Oh no, Mr. Page! It's all splendid! It's just that I'm getting rather nervous as the lady is due any moment. Do carry on!

WALTER. Thank you. Right. I may proceed with our final rehearsal?

MARCIA. Please Mr. Page ...

WALTER. (*He goes again to the sofa and points a warning finger at the pile of cushions. Slight pause.*)Where was I?

MARCIA. Ocular proof.

WALTER. Thank you. You had better been born a dog than ... than get me going like this! (*Very long pause. He tugs his trousers down an inch and puts his hand inside his jacket to ease his armpit. He points to the cushions with slow deliberation and turns to MARCIA and speaks slowly and distinctly.*) Now for your benefit, madam, and to make totally sure you know what is happening. This lady is now *probably* telling me more details of how she saw you with her husband. I will walk slowly to the window and stare out. (*He does so. Pause.*)

MARCIA. Is she still speaking?

WALTER. Yes. (*A beat.*) She has now finished. (*Into the part.*) I warn you, Mrs. Erskine, that if you slander her pray no more. Abandon all remorse! Understand this, madam, I think my wife is honest. So I must have some proof! The name of my dear wife ... my dear ... (*In normal tone.*) ... what's your name again? (*He snaps his fingers ...*)

MARCIA. Marcia.

WALTER. (*Resumes.*) The name of my dear wife, my dear Marcia is, to me, valued above rubies!

MARCIA. Do excuse me, Mr. Page. What does "Abandon all remorse" mean?

WALTER. Madam! One more interruption and I shall leave the building! (*Pause.*) Thank you. (*He turns away ... sobs.*) I would have been happy if the whole of Knightsbridge had tasted her sweet body and I had not known. But now ... for ever ... farewell the tranquil mind! Farewell content! Farewell ... my increased exports ... my victorious shareholders' meetings ... all the things that made my ambition a virtue. How could you have done this to me, Monica?

MARCIA. Marcia.

WALTER. Sod it. Marcia! ... Marcia! Marcia! Yes. Got it now ... let me see your eyes ...(*He goes to her and lifts her chin.*) Let me see your face. Oh God! You are as false as hell! Impudent strumpet! (*He goes to slap her face but she turns away too soon and he misses her as she claps her hands.*) No! No! No! You keep turning too soon, you stupid nana!

MARCIA. If I don't, you'll hit me!

WALTER. We've been over this all afternoon, madam. Only when you feel my hand coming do you turn sharply to the right and clap your hand! I missed you by a yard then!

MARCIA. But I don't want to be hit!

WALTER. I will not hit you if you do as I say! Take the timing from me! When I say "right" turn and clap. (*Pulls his trousers down an inch.*)

MARCIA. Couldn't I just burst into tears and run into the bedroom?

WALTER. *After* I have slapped you, madam. This is what she has come for! This is what she expects me to do! We have to put on a show! I can't seem to get that into your head, madam.

MARCIA. I'm sorry. I'll take my time from you.

WALTER. Thank you. (*He goes back to the sofa. Declaims.*) Let me see your face! Oh God! You are as false as hell! Impudent strumpet! (*He goes to slap her ...*) Now! (*He hits her.*)

MARCIA. How dare you! (*She rubs her face.*)

WALTER. (*Patiently.*) You were too *late* that time, madam.

MARCIA. I was waiting for you to say "right". (*Sniffs a real tear.*)

WALTER. I did. (*Stares out, not looking at her.*)

MARCIA. You didn't. You said "now!". I've never been struck in my life! (*She looks in the mirror.*) I shall have a terrible red mark there! Quite honestly, Mr. Page, I see no reason why you have to hit me!

WALTER. If you could only do what I tell you, madam, my hand would pass three inches in front of your nose! When I played ... whatshis name at whatsthatplace ... when was it? I was slapped every night and not once was I struck!

MARCIA. Couldn't I just pretend to burst into tears when you say "impudent strumpet" then rush into my bedroom?

WALTER. (*Sighs, then very dignified.*) Very well, madam. It won't be *nearly* so good, but I suppose I must, finally, accept the limitations of my material. (*He pulls down the crotch of his trousers.*) It's the story of my life. I'm always working with rubbish. Seven years ago, on the opening night of *Private Lives* at Darlington ... I received an ovation at the end of the first act. An ovation. All the critics were in and I knew I was giving the performance of my life. I was in my dressing room during that first interval ... glowing with ecstasy. Then as I made my entrance in the second act, the door stuck and I had to come through the fireplace. The audience was totally bemused. Naturally. There's no Father Christmas in *Private Lives*. Story of my life. No matter how good I am ... there's always someone who drags me down. (*He stretches his mouth.*)

MARCIA. But I am delighted with the way you're helping me, Mr. Page. I think you're absolutely splendid as my husband!

WALTER. You are too kind, madam. (*Looks at his watch.*) Shall we just have a final briefing of what we do when the lady arrives?

MARCIA. You will leave the flat then arrive ten minutes later as if you've just flown in. We will let her spill the beans. I shall then say I'm going away to give you time to think things over. I shall leave you to get rid of her on your own and phone you half an hour later. If you answer, I'll say wrong number and ring off. If you don't answer, she's gone.

WALTER. Excellent. You have a better grasp of the mechanics of the scene than of the emotional content, but with a fair wind we might just make it.

MARCIA. I'm really grateful to you. I think it's just wonderful the way you've stepped into the breach like this.

WALTER. (*Declaims.*) Once more into the breach and fill up the whole with our English dead! Ha! Ah! What a speech! You know? I am not given to personal vanity but I would have been a superb Henry the Fifth. Too old now of course. I used to recite the Agincourt speech as I was making up the wage packets for the North Thames Gas Board! Suddenly I wasn't sitting in the depot before two gasometers in West Drayton ... I was in the battle field of France before Harfleur. Alarms! Enter King Henry and Soldiers with scaling ladders. Once more unto the breach, dear friends, once more: or close the wall up with our English dead! In peace there's nothing so becomes a man as modest stillness and humility; but when the blast of war blows in our ears, then initiate the action of the tiger, stiffen the sinews ... (*He leaps up on a chair.*) summon up the blood.

MARCIA. Excuse me, Mr. Page, but that is a very valuable chair.

WALTER. Disguise fair nature with hard-favour'd rage: (*MARCIA scratches.*) Then lend the eye a terrible aspect. Now set the teeth, and stretch the nostril wide: hold hard the breath, and bend up every spirit to his full height! On, on ... (*She scratches again.*)

MARCIA. Please Mr. Page.

WALTER. On, on you noble English ... now attest that those whom you call'd fathers did beget you! And you, good yeoman, whose limbs were made in England, show us here the mettle of your pasture. I see you stand like greyhounds in the slips. straining upon the start. The game's afoot: Follow your spirit; and, upon this charge, Cry 'God for Harry, England, and Saint George!' (*As his feet go through the chair, splintering the seat, the doorbell rings.*)

MARCIA. Oh God!

WALTER. First positions everybody! (*As he struggles out of the chair MARCIA helps him. WALTER runs into the study. MARCIA looks at the chair and puts a magazine over the broken seat. She goes into the hall and opens the door to JANE who is delighted with MARCIA'S obvious distress.*)

JANE. Oh good evening, Mrs. Hornbeam. Have I come at a convenient time?

MARCIA. Yes er ... er ... Do come in ... (*JANE enters the sitting room.*)

JANE. Thank you. What a charming apartment.

MARCIA. Thank you. My husband has not arrived yet but I expect him any moment. You won't have to wait long.

JANE. Oh good. I know he's coming back some time this evening. I phone your husband's secretary and she expects him in the office first thing tomorrow. I discovered he is chairman of Atlas Folk Lift Trucks. Wasn't that clever of me?

MARCIA. It was.

(*WALTER quietly opens the study door and pads to the front door. Carrying a suitcase and a paper bag. He opens the front door and puts his cases outside, then puts a key in the lock and closes the front door without a sound.*)

JANE. I didn't tell *her* any detail, of course.

MARCIA. Thank you. I appreciate that.

JANE. I just said I wanted to speak to him urgently on a private matter.

MARCIA. I'm very grateful.

JANE. You expect him soon you say?

MARCIA. Any moment. He phoned from London Airport an hour ago. Mrs. Erskine, could I just ask you one thing? Are you quite determined to tell Reggie?

JANE. Quite determined.

MARCIA. I only ask because Reggie and i have an old fashioned marriage and he is almost sure to divorce me. Even if he doesn't, your information will have a dreadful effect on the rest of our lives together.

JANE. Your affair with Brian is going to have a dreadful effect on the rest of *my* married life.

MARCIA. Then I can't dissuade you?

JANE. Awfully sorry.

MARCIA. (*Smiles thinly.*) Then we need say no more. Do sit down ... I'll make some tea?

JANE. Thank you.

(*MARCIA exits into the kitchen.*
JANE goes to sit on the sofa but then sees that the seat consists only of rubber straps. She hesitates and goes to the easy chair. This has the same seating arrangements. She frowns at this odd style and looks down at the easy chair again. She presses one of the rubber straps. She still hesitates but then finally, gingerly, sits in the chair. For five seconds it

appears OK, but then she leans back and crosses her legs and drops through the seat. She is now trapped with her bottom on the floor and with two of the rubber straps tightly round either side of her waist. For a moment she cannot move then heaves herself up by the arms.She finally stands, surveys the other two matching pieces and goes to the cane chair, and as she reaches for the magazine ...)

MARCIA. (*From the kitchen.*) But perhaps you'd prefer a drink, Mrs. Erskine?

JANE. (*Looks back to the kitchen as she takes the magazine.*) No thank you. Tea would be perfect. (*She stands for a moment fliting through the magazine then sits on the chair. Her bottom goes right through it and her legs shoot up and splay out either side of it. This time she cannot get out.*)

MARCIA. (*Comes in with a tray and sets it down on the dining table chatting brightly and not looking in JANE's direction.*) I agree. There's nothing like a cup of tea is there? I've made a pot of Indian and China so we can have either. I'm going to treat myself to some of these absolute divine jaffa cakes which are fiendishly fattening but irresistible. I do hope you will join me. How would you like it? Indian with milk or lemon or some of my Lapsong Souchong? (*She turns to the easy chair and then sees JANE struggling and gives a strangled hoot.*) Oh dear! I am sorry! I should have warned you about that chair! I'm frightfully sorry! Do let me help you! (*MARCIA goes to JANE who is clutching the sides. Slight pause.*) What do you think is best?

JANE. I haven't the slightest idea.

MARCIA. Actually, I wish Reggie were here now. (*Slight pause.*) He's so good at this sort of thing. He's frightfully practical. Anyway, we can't leave you like that! It'll confuse Reggie dreadfully. It'll also put him in a terrible temper. That chair was given to him by his aunt on her death bed.

JANE. I didn't break it. I simply sat on it and went through.

MARCIA. Well hold on now ... I was a Girl Guide once an got a proficiency badge for enterprise at summer camp. How would it be if I held your legs while you pushed up?

JANE. Yes that might do it.

MARCIA. Right. (*She presses on JANE's knees which are over the edge of the chair.*) Now ... You push up! (*JANE pushes herself up.*) Wonderful! Now give me your hand. Now! (*As JANE releases one hand, MARCIA releases both her hands and JANE drops even further down and is wedged.*)

MARCIA. Ah! Now just a moment. I think we'd better go back to the drawing board, as Reggie always says. What a pretty slip! Is it Janet Reger?

JANE. Please do something, Mrs. Hornbeam!
I'm being suffocated by my own knee caps!
(*MARCIA pushes the chair over onto its side and
waggles the chair from JANE.*)

MARCIA. Awfully sorry about this.

JANE. (*Rises and brushes herself down.*) My
tights are ruined!

MARCIA. But I must say ... you are
frightfully supple aren't you? Do you do yoga? I
think I'd better put this in the spare room. I don't
want him to see it the *moment* he comes in.

JANE. I didn't break it.

MARCIA. No ... no ... I did ... standing on it
to adjust my curtain runners. I'll take it out of
sight. If he sees his one and only Chippendale
chair like this while you're telling him the details
of my adultery, I think it will be the straw that
broke the camel's back! (*She takes the chair out to
the study and looks round. She opens the
cloakroom door to make sure WALTER has gone.
She looks at her watch and returns to the sitting
room.*) He's got a terrible Welsh temper as it is.

JANE. Yes, they said in Who's Who he was
born in Wales.

MARCIA. And he's never lost his accent. (*She
realizes.*) I mean he's never lost his *love* of the
Welsh accent. He himself hasn't got a Welsh
accent at all!

JANE. I've always like the Celts. Is that your
wedding photograph on the piano?

MARCIA. Oh God! (*She goes to it immediately.*) I'd better put that away! That'll make him *very* emotional. (*She takes it out to the kitchen.*)

JANE. Mrs. Hornbeam, could I ask *you* just one question?

MARCIA. By all means. (*She appears in the arch.*)

JANE. Is your affair with Brian over?

MARCIA. Yes. (*Slight pause.*) But why should you believe me?

JANE. I had lunch with Brian today, he said it was over.

MARCIA. Oh really?

JANE. But I'd believe you more than him.

MARCIA. You've told him you've seen me?

JANE. Yes. I phoned up his golf club on a hunch and they said he was out on the links. So as he was about to make a shot in some long grass I sprang up from behind a bush.

MARCIA. He must have been surprised?

JANE. I think so. His ball landed in the pond. But then we had a very nice lunch in the club house. He said that when I caught him last night it was a farewell supper.

MARCIA. That is true. Neither of us said as much but we both knew.

JANE. And you're not going to see each other again?

MARCIA. No. We had a brief infatuation ... but it was purely physical and we exhausted it on holiday.

JANE. (*Noble.*) I am prepared to accept that, Mrs. Hornbeam.

MARCIA. Thank you. (*Pause.*) Does this mean you've decided not to tell Reggie?

JANE. Oh no! I have to tell Reggie. But I will tell him that I believe the relationship is now over.

MARCIA. I see. (*A beat.*) Thank you.

JANE. I want to be fair, Mrs. Hornbeam. Well, we have nothing else to say to each other so I'll go now and come back about ten.

MARCIA. What? No! Please! You can't go! Reggie will really be home then. I mean he'll be here any moment!

JANE. I know but I've decided to let you tell him your version first. I'm making this concession because I'm prepared to believe that your relationship with my husband really is over and I don't want to make it *too* bad for you. (*She goes to the door.*)

MARCIA. No please Mrs. Erskine! I don't want to tell Reggie my version first ... (*Then desperately.*) Oh God! Look, before you go ... (*JANE stops at the sitting room door.*)

JANE. Yes?

MARCIA. Could I tell you something in confidence? (*She scratches violently.*) Something about myself ... something very personal ...? (*JANE looks at MARCIA scratching.*)

JANE. You haven't caught anything have you?

MARCIA. What?

JANE. Something you might have give to Brian which he might pass on to me? (*JANE scratches absently.*)

MARCIA. I haven't caught anything.

JANE. Then why are you scratching?

MARCIA. My nervous rash. It's not contagious.

JANE. Oh good. (*Slight pause.*) What do you wish to tell me, Mrs. Hornbeam?

MARCIA. It's terribly important.

JANE. Yes?

MARCIA. (*Rises and discreetly looks at her watch as she goes to look out of the window.*) It is this ... (*Her mind a total blank.*) Simply this. (*Pause.*) I just want to say this and I won't keep you a moment longer.

JANE. Yes? (*Pause.*)

MARCIA. Last night ...

JANE. Yes?

MARCIA. When you saw me in that restaurant. (*She scratches.*)

JANE. Yes?

MARCIA. I was sitting by the window ...

JANE. With my husband ... yes?

MARCIA. Correct. (*A beat.*) Absolutely correct. I don't deny it. I was sitting in the window of that restaurant with your husband. Spot

on. There was no mistake. I was sitting in the
window of that restaurant with your husband.

JANE. Which is why I'm here. I'll pop back
around eight.

MARCIA. Ah yes ... but there is something
you don't know.

JANE. What?

MARCIA. (*Looks at the clock. A beat.*) You
say you saw me last night in the window of that
restaurant with your husband?

JANE. We have established that surely?

MARCIA. But ... and this is the big but ...

JANE. Yes?

MARCIA. You say you saw us eating creme
brulees?

JANE. Yes.

MARCIA. No.

JANE. No what?

MARCIA. On that point you are totally wrong.

JANE. What point?

MARCIA. They were crepe suzettes.

JANE. Yes?

MARCIA. We were *not eating* creme brulees!

JANE. So?

MARCIA. Ah! Yes! So. You may well say
that. (*Pause.*) Yes. Well, now, to get to the crunch.
(*Goes to the window and looks out.*)

JANE. Yes?

MARCIA. Did your friend describe me to you
when she first saw me?

JANE. Yes.

MARCIA. How did she describe me?

JANE. Why go into that? The description was not very flattering ... naturally. She's my friend!

MARCIA. Please ... do tell me exactly what she said about me?

JANE. I can't see what bearing ...?

MARCIA. Please ...

JANE. It'll only upset you and I think you're in quite a state already.

MARCIA. Please ... I won't mind ... Please tell me. It's very important to me. Tell me. Take your time, but tell me everything.

JANE. Well, first she said you wore rather too much make-up.

MARCIA. (*Immediately.*) The saucy bitch!

JANE. Look, I don't really want to discuss my friend ... or her description of you. (*She opens the door. MARCIA now desperately playing for time.*)

MARCIA. No! No! She's right ... and that is the whole point!

JANE. What?

MARCIA. I hate to admit this ... I can't tell you how I hate to admit this.

JANE. Yes?

MARCIA. I have to say it!

JANE. What?

MARCIA. I *was* wearing too much make-up! (*Pause.*)

JANE. That is the important thing you have to tell me?

MARCIA. (*Pause. Then defeated.*) Yes.

JANE. I'm sorry you have make-up problems, but at this moment I have to say, Mrs. Hornbeam, it is not of consuming interest to me! I'll be back later this evening. (*Turns to the door.*)

MARCIA. No please ... you can't go out on a dark wet night like this!

JANE. It's not dark or raining.

MARCIA. No really, I can't let you just go out and walk the street for three hours!

JANE. I'm going home to cook Brian his supper then I'm coming back.

MARCIA. No ... you are only going because I've been so inhospitable. How very rude of me! Do have some tea!

JANE. No thank you.

MARCIA. I must make you welcome. Let me entertain you till Reggie comes! (*She sits at the piano and begins to play CLEMENTINE, then EARLY ONE MORNING,* which she sings in a wavery contralto:*)

EARLY ONE MORNING
JUST AS THE SUN WAS RISING
I HEARD A MAIDEN SINGING ...
IN THE VALLEY BELOW ...
OH PLEASE NEVER LEAVE ME
OH PLEASE DON'T DECEIVE ME ...
HOW COULD YOU TREAT A POOR

---

* See Music Note, p. 4

MAIDEN SO?
(*Pause.*)

JANE. That's very charming, Mrs. Hornbeam, but I really must go ...

MARCIA. (Now *plays and sings louder.*) Rule Britannia! Britannia rules the waves! Britain never never never shall (*MARCIA screams. JANE goes out into the hall. JANE runs back in ... MARCIA puts her fingers to her lips.*) Look! (*She crooks her finger to beckon JANE to the window. JANE cautiously, goes to the window.*) Out there! It's absolutely fascinating!

JANE. (*Looks out.*) What?

MARCIA. In the square! The most beautiful thing I've ever seen.

JANE. All I can see is two dogs copulating.

MARCIA. (*Looks.*) What! Ah! Yes. There you are! It goes on everywhere!

JANE. I should have a nice lie down, Mrs. Hornbeam and I'll see you later. (*She turns to go.*)

MARCIA. Please don't leave me alone. I'll go mad! My Spanish dancing! (*Runs to sideboard and rummages and takes out some castenettes.*) I go every Tuesday evening!

(*She puts a cassette on and strikes a pose. She dances, swishing her skirt round JANE.*
WALTER enters, stops, bemused then enters living room with his cases. For some moments MARCIA dances unaware then sees

*him and that he now wears a moustache and a
bowler hat.)*

JANE. Mr. Hornbeam?
MARCIA. Oooh! Reggie! My God! That
moustache! You didn't tell me about the
moustache!

*(She gives a gurgle of surpressed, hysterical
laughter then runs into the bedroom and
slams the door.*
*WALTER has a suspicious moment. He carries
the case, the Pan-Am overnight bag, and a
copy of the Financial Times.)*

WALTER. Marcia? *(He looks at JANE, then
at sitting room.)* What's happening? Who are
you? *(Now has an Edward Heath type of accent.)*
Is my wife all right?
JANE. It's Mr. Hornbeam isn't it?
WALTER. Er ... yes ... excuse me a moment
... *(He goes to the bedroom and eases his collar.)*
Marcia? *(The bedroom door opens.)*
MARCIA. Look Reggie ... *(She goes bug-eyed
again and slams the door. JANE closes the front
door and comes into the room. WALTER puts
down his bags.)*
WALTER. What's going on? *(He tugs his
trousers in the crotch. Then removes his hat and
puts down the bag.)*

JANE. My name is Jane Erskine, Mr. Hornbeam.

WALTER. I'm sorry ... do I know you?

JANE. No, we haven't met.

WALTER. I er ... er ... just a moment please. (*He tries to open the bedroom door. It is locked. He knocks on it.*) Marcia, what the *hell's* going on? (*Pause. MARCIA opens the door. In the slight interval she has mussed up her hair and made her face pale. She looks at WALTER rigid with determination not to explode and from now on pointedly avoids looking at him.*)

MARCIA. Please tell him why you are here, Mrs. Erskine.

JANE. Very well! I've been waiting for you to get home, Mr. Hornbeam, in order to tell you that your wife has been having an affair with my husband ten days a year for the past three years.

(*WALTER gives his "stunned" look, which consists of very raised eyebrows and an open mouth. This is something we have not seen him do before, and as he looks at MARCIA she is quite startled by it and goes glassy eyed suppressing her giggles.*)

MARCIA. Oooh! (*With the same expression he looks at JANE. A beat. Then back to MARCIA. The pause is four times too long.*)

WALTER. Pardon?

JANE. This year they had a holiday in Capri. For ten days. While you were away in the Middle East.

WALTER. Pardon?

JANE. Brian has also told me that he went to Morocco with her last year and Crete the year before. He told me all this because last night I saw him with your wife, holding hands in a restaurant and today he admitted everything.

WALTER. I see. (*Pause. MARCIA returns. He looks at both then goes slowly to the drinks tray and pours himself a large one.*) I need a large brandy.

MARCIA. (*Immediately.*) Reggie doesn't drink! (*To JANE.*) He doesn't drink normally.

WALTER. But I'm having one now! Do you mind! (*WALTER is genuinely cross.*)

MARCIA. No, of course not! It's your house. You can do exactly what you like. It's just that you haven't touched a drop for years.

WALTER. I assume it is true what this lady has just told me about you and her husband fornicating in Capri?

MARCIA. Yes.

WALTER. And you are surprised I want a drink!

MARCIA. (*Nervously.*) I'm sorry ... do have a drink. Let's all have one. I could do with one. I could do with a couple! (*WALTER pours two large brandies and hands them to JANE and MARCIA.*)

JANE. Thank you. My name is Jane, by the way. (*A beat.*) I'm sorry to have given you such a nasty home coming, Mr. Hornbeam.

WALTER. Please call me ... (*Dries.*) .. Just call me ...(*Faces his collar and tugs his sleeve and trousers.*)

MARCIA. (*Realizes at last.*) Shall we all sit down *Reggie!*

WALTER. Yes .. just call me Reggie. I'm so stunned. I just can't believe this is happening!

JANE. I do understand, Reggie. I was like that myself last night when my friend phoned me and said she'd seen them together. I couldn't believe it either, Brian had told me he'd gone to Scotland to fish for ten days. Last year he told me he'd gone to America on business for ten days. *And* the year before that! And suddenly to realize ... that he'd been lying to me for so long ... I just couldn't believe it. Then I went to the restaurant and saw for myself ... I just stood there, totally stunned. Just like you are now!

WALTER. It has gone on for three years! (*MARCIA goes to the window and does not see WALTER takes out some glasses and put them on.*)

MARCIA. But there is one thing Mrs. Erskine has omitted to mention, Reggie. (*She stares out.*) It is this ...(*She turns and catches his spectacles and smothers an immediate, compulsive hoot of mirth in her throat and changes it to a bout of coughing.*) Pardon! (*She turns back to the window and coughs. She stops and opens her mouth but coughs again. She tightens her face and tries desperately to control herself.*) It is thi ...(*Her voice wavers dangerously. She stops. Bites her lip.*) Good bye ... last night ... do tell him please? Mrs. Ers ... (*She gives up, being unable to maintain a sober demeanor.*)

JANE. Your wife and my husband *have* said that last night *was* a farewell supper and that they are never going to see each other again. It didn't look like a goodbye supper to *me* as I watched them holding hands over the table, but I am prepared to accept that they *might* be telling the truth. That, of course, does not affect what has gone on in the past.

WALTER. You have had an affair with Joan's husband for three years!?

JANE. Jane ...

WALTER. You have had Jane's husband here for ten days every September while I was in America?

MARCIA. (*Muted but still not turning.*) No - not here. We've been away. She's just *told* you that!

WALTER. Don't take that tone with me, you tart.

MARCIA. I'm very sorry, Reggie. (*She turns but avoids looking at him.*) I do love you, Reggie. Always have. Always will.

WALTER. But all the years we've been together ... the love and trust we have shared! My

God! (He strides up and down as he gets into the swing of it.) I feel ... I feel as if I've had a kick in the stomach! My whole life is collapsing round me! How could you betray me like this! How dare you!

MARCIA. *(Sharply.)* Well don't go on! *(She realizes instantly that this bold tone is a mistake.)* Yes, of course, you must go on. You have every *right* to go on. My behaviour has been ... been ... *(Pause.)*

WALTER. *(Helping her out.)* Appalling! *(Eases his trousers.)*

MARCIA. Yes ... appalling and I can't defend it ...

WALTER. Oh God! I never expected this when I got home! How could you, Moira?

MARCIA. Oh Reggie ... please don't call me Moira. It'll make me cry. You haven't called Moira since that first time you said you loved me! And I corrected you and you said I looked like a Moira to you! Please *don't* call me Moira, Reggie ... it upsets me so much! Just Marcia ... please ... *(She gives him a steely look and scratches herself.)*

WALTER. Very well Marcia ...*(He puts his hand inside his jacket to ease the armpit.)*

MARCIA. Yes ... I did have a brief infatuation with Brian, but it is now over ... done with forever. I have never stopped loving *you*, even so ... I know I have to be punished, Mr. Page.

WALTER. Please don't call me Mr. Page. Those wonderful early days when we were so much in love and you said I looked like a Mr. Page to you, those days are gone for *ever!*

MARCIA. Reggie! Oh my God ... please ... look ... punish me ... give me a black eye if you like! I'd accept it with pleasure ... I would! Just give me a good punch in the eye ... if it'd make you feel better ...

WALTER. (*Genuinely baffled.*) You *want* me to give you a black eye?

MARCIA. (*Hastily.*) I don't *want* a black eye, naturally, but if you feel it would help you ease your anger ... your bitter disappointment, then I would accept it and still love you. (*WALTER gives his "baffled outrage" look.*) I don't care what you do to me, just as long ...(*She catches his look and starts to go again. She turns hastily to the window.*) ... as long as you stop looking at me like that. You don't know what it does to me, Reggie! (*She gives another strangled spasm of volcanic mirth then coughs ...*) Anything, Reggie ... but don't look like that! (*She runs into the bedroom and shuts the door. Pause. He goes to the door. It is locked. He bangs on it ...*)

WALTER. Come out of there you impudent strumpet! I haven't finished with you! I haven't even *started!* How dare you walk out on me! (*Bangs again. Silence.*) Oh God! Had heaven been pleased to afflict me: had they rain'd all kinds of sores and shames on my bare head:

Steeped me in poverty to the very lips ...
imprisoned me ... I should have found in some
place of my heart a drop of patience: but to make
me a figure of scorn ... (*Bangs on the door.*) Open
this door you whore! (*The door opens. MARCIA
opens it, takes one look at his face and gives a
shriek of hysterical laughter then slams the door
again.*)

WALTER. How dare you?! (*He is genuinely
furious and pounds on the door .. then picks up a
vase.*)

JANE. Oh please Reggie ... (*She runs to him
and holds his arm.*) ... don't do anything you'll
regret. I'm sure that's Dresden. She's not
laughing at *you!* She wouldn't dare laugh at *you!* I
don't want you to hurt her, Reggie! I never meant
that. I just wanted to tell you ... She's so terrified
... It's only hysterics ... please Reggie ... She's
hysterical! She's not laughing at you, I'm sure. I
can't be responsible for two breakages in one day!
It's hysteria, Reggie. I promise you.

WALTER. I see. I'm sorry ... I ... don't know
what I'm doing. I come back from Bahrain ... I'm
still jet lagged ... I walk in and my life is
finished!

JANE. Do please sit down, Reggie. You've
gone awfully red in the face.

WALTER. I will, thank you ... (*He sits on the
sofa quite normally.*)

JANE. Is that all right to sit on ...?

WALTER. What have I done to her to deserve this? I've never deprived her of anything. She's got an entire wardrobe of fur coats! Anything she has wanted from me I've gladly given ... Gladly! Because she is my life. She is my life, Joanna.

JANE. Jane.

WALTER. I'm not capable of giving her any more! I've given her everything I have to give. (*His face crumples into tears and he covers his face in his hands.*)

JANE. Oh Reggie ... oh please ... I can't bear to see a man cry. Oh please Reggie ... I never realized ... I knew you'd be cross ... yes ... I wanted you to be furious with her ... as I was furious with Brian. I would have been delighted if you had given her a black eye but that is all I wanted, that would have been the end of it ... but not this, Reggie! Oh please ... (*He sobs silently. She sits gingerly on the edge of the sofa.*) Please Reggie ... Please Reggie ... I never thought you would take it as badly as this! I'm not going to divorce Brian. I still love him. I shall give him a dreadful time for the next six months ... yes ... but I still love him! (*WALTER lets out a muffled sob.*)

JANE. Oh please Reggie ... don't ... please don't ... (*She puts her arm around him and goes back on the sofa.*) I feel so terrible ...(*She sinks with a cry between the rubber straps so that her head is now level with his waist and her bottom on the floor. He turns and sees where she is and is immediately alert.)*

WALTER. For Christ's sake! (*He rises and yanks her out, and speaks in his normal off-London accent.*) Do I have to do *everything* myself round here! Stage managers they call themselves. They couldn't manage a piss up in a brewery! (*He takes the bust to the sideboard and resumes his performance.*) My wife is such a dreadful housekeeper. She piles everything up to dust the furniture then she leaves it there! I am so sorry! (*He distributes the cushions back to the sofa and chairs.*) Do have a cushion.

JANE. Thank you. (*He slides it under her. MARCIA comes out wearing a jacket and carrying a small bag.*)

WALTER. And apart from anything else, Mabel ... this flat looks a tip! I've just travelled half way round the world and when I get home I have to do the housework!

MARCIA. I'm very sorry, Reggie ... but I won't trouble you any more with my presence. I'm leaving you.

WALTER. You are leaving *me!*

MARCIA. I think it is for the best, Reggie. It'll give you time to think things over ... besides, I cannot bear to discuss my marriage in front of this woman for another moment. I'd just like to remind you that you have a dinner engagement with that Government minister at eight so you must leave soon. I shall ring you in a few days,

Reggie, and no doubt you will tell me then whether you wish me to remain your wife. Meanwhile you'd probably like your ring back. The one you bought me for our last wedding anniversary. This lovely cabochon ruby! Here! Take it! (*She takes it off and throws it on the chair and with a stifled sob, walks out.*)

WALTER. (*Collects the ring.*) Oh God ... where was I? Oh yes! Yes, I would have been happy if the whole of Knightsbridge barracks has tasted her sweet body and I hadn't known, Penny. But now for ever ... farewell the tranquil mind ... what use are rubies? Just lying trinkets for a strumpet's momentary pleasure. Take this worthless bauble from me ...(*He tosses it aside not looking, unaware of the direction. It lands on the sofa next to JANE.*)

JANE. Really? O no ... you can't mean that, Reggie. Goodness me ... you can't ... surely? Do you really mean that? It is nice ... It's lovely, in fact. I've never had a ring like this. Really is ... Do you mind if I have a closer look? (*Takes out jewelers' eyeglass from handbag.*) I'm in the trade, you see. And it fits like a dream! So sweet of you, Reggie! (*She examines it on her hand ...*)

WALTER. Oh God ... that I should live to see such betrayal! Farewell the tranquil ...

JANE. (*Briskly.*) No look, Reggie, there's no need to go on being upset. You've now been told the worse so that's it! You now know and I know so

let's lick our wounds and discuss what we intend
to do about it.

WALTER. No ... no ... I haven't finished ...

JANE. But there's no point in moping about it,
Reggie! So let's ...

WALTER. No! I have to say ... *Please* ...
permit me to say ... finally ... that it were better to
be born a dog than suffer ... (*He eases his finger
inside his collar.*) ... the damn laundries play
hell with my shirts. Would you mind if I slipped
into something more casual?

JANE. I don't mind Reggie but aren't you
leaving shortly to dine with some Government
minister?

WALTER. I shall cancel. (*Dials phone. Then
into phone.*) Sir James Ottaway please. Walter.
Reggie Hornbeam. (*A beat.*) Hello Jimmy ... just
a quick word. Must cancel tonight. Got a domestic
crisis. Yes I got a ten million order in Bahrain.
We'll speak later. Bye. (*Hangs up.*) That's that
done. I am at your disposal for as long as you
like.

JANE. How nice! Yes ... well we might as
well make ourselves comfortable while we decide
the future of our respective marriages.

WALTER. That's what I thought.

JANE. May *I* take off my shoes?

WALTER. Please do. ... (*He goes into the
bedroom. She goes to the window and looks out,
then returns to the sofa and arranges herself in a
decorous position. WALTER comes out wearing a*

silk dressing gown with a polka dot scarf at the neck. He is obviously no stranger to quick changes.)

JANE. Do you still love her, Reggie?

WALTER. (*He puts both hands in the pockets with his thumbs out.*) Totally ... utterly ... bitterly! (*Gradually his Darlington performance of Noel Coward takes over. He goes slowly and elegantly to get a drink.*) And I shall continue to love her till my dying day. (*He turns to her.*) I have been in love with her from the very first moment I set eyes on her!

JANE. Oh dear! I am sorry Reggie. You look so hurt. I feel quite beastly.

WALTER. No need to my dear. I shall always be very grateful to you for showing me what a damn fool I've been! May I freshen your glass? (*He pours her another drink.*)

JANE. You know Reggie ... I think you're a romantic like me.

WALTER. Yes. A romantic ass!

JANE. Where did you first meet her?

WALTER. At a house party in Norfolk, (*Goes to window.*) She looked so ravishing in that damn moonlight!

JANE. Oh how beautiful that you should remember the moonlight! I bet you even remember the first words you spoke together?

WALTER. How could I ever forget?

JANE. What were they? (*He is stymied for a moment but then shuts his eyes as he tries to remember the lines.*)

WALTER. She was looking out over the balcony ... quite alone and looking so perfectly adorable ... I watched her for a long time, plucking up my courage ... then finally I went to her and said "Very flat, Norfolk." She turned and smiled and said ... "Well don't look at me. I'm even flatter!"

JANE. Oh really? (*This is not the romantic exchange she expected.*)

WALTER. I was enchanted by her from that moment on! (*He drifts to the piano.*) Look here, Verity ... my nerves are in such tiny pieces ... would you mind if I played something? I'd find it so soothing!

JANE. Oh yes! Please do, Reggie. I find music very soothing myself.

WALTER. (*He sits at the piano and plays a few bars of "I'll See You Again"** , *and then, still playing, he looks at her.*) Do you still love ... whatshisname?

JANE. Brian? Oh yes! Enormously!

WALTER. Isn't it damnable! (*He continues to play quietly.*)

JANE. I love him so much, I couldn't possibly hurt him the way he has hurt me.

---

* See Music Note, p. 4

WALTER. Exactly what I was thinking about er ... yes. (*Then very clipped.*) You've taken the very words right out of my mouth! Isn't it astonishing how cheap music is so potent! (*He plays a wrong note and immediately concentrates on his playing.*)

JANE. (*A delicate conjecture.*) And yet Reggie ... I feel they should be hurt a *little!* Don't you?

WALTER. I er ... (*He stops in the middle of a bar.*)

JANE. Oh please don't stop Reggie. You play so beautifully and it's so poignant that you should play that particular song. It's not cheap to me. It brings back so many happy memories of my early days with Brian. Do go on ... please. (*He does not go on from where he left off but begins the song from the beginning again.*) I don't know what *you* feel, of course ... but personally ... I feel we owe it to ourselves to do *something* in response, even just a little something.

WALTER. (*He looks up.*) Really! (*He plays another song. Looks down again.*)

JANE. But what? (*She looks at him.*) That's the problem. I suppose I could avenge my hurt feelings by rushing out and have some sordid affair. That would hurt Brian.

WALTER. Quite.

JANE. But it wouldn't help your injured feelings would it?

WALTER. I'm sorry? (*He stops and restarts playing.*)

JANE. It wouldn't help you get your own back on Marcia. (*Hastily.*) Not that I' d dream of doing anything just for revenge!

WALTER. Quite.

JANE. That would be just mean and petty. Demeaning for both of us.

WALTER. Quite.

JANE. We don't want *revenge*.

WALTER. No!

JANE. But I do feel they should suffer in *some* way.

WALTER. Quite.

JANE. Particularly Marcia. (*He stops playing at exactly the same point as before.*)

JANE. You don't agree?

WALTER. I do.

JANE. Well don't stop, Reggie. You play with such feeling. (*He starts the song again from the beginning and it is now apparent that he only knows up to this point.*) It would be the same for me if you went out and deliberately had an affair, merely to get your own back on Marcia. It wouldn't hurt Brian would it?

WALTER. I'd fail anyway. I'm not very attractive to women. (*She looks at him, astonished, as he concentrates on a few bars he has had slight trouble with earlier.*)

JANE. How *can* you say that, Reggie?! That's incredible! (*She arranges her dress to show more of her legs.*) A man in your position! Chairman of Atlas Fork Lift Trucks! Don't you know that men with power are irresistible to women!

WALTER. I can only tell you my dear, ... in the past twenty years I have never seen a woman look at me with anything *remotely* resembling physical desire.

JANE. They must have, Reggie!

WALTER. No. Women look at me as if I was some butcher delivering a pound of liver.

JANE. That can't possibly be true, Reggie! You're rich, successful ... you control a great empire! Of course women fancy you!

WALTER. (*A rueful smile.*) You're very kind my dear.

JANE. But I mean it! Hundreds of women must have made themselves available to you!

WALTER. I can only say, that if they have, I wish they had made it a *little* more obvious.

JANE. Oh Reggie ... You're so lovely! I never expected you to be like this!

WALTER. Like what?

JANE. So completely devoid of personal vanity. All your power ... your money ... the fact that you control the destinies of thousands of people ... I felt sure you'd be a smooth man of the world. Strong man, confident ... authoritative ...

WALTER. All my confidence has gone tonight.

JANE. (*Rises and puts her hands on his shoulders.*) You know, Reggie ... it's because you are so humble, so totally devoid of personal pride, that you have never noticed the dozens of women who *must* fling themselves at you. I find that very endearing, Reggie ... (*She goes and drapes herself on the piano.*)

WALTER. I swear to you. I haven't had an offer from a lady since my twice-nightly summer season at Colwyn Bay.

JANE. Since what?

WALTER. (*Realizing.*) I was visiting one of my depots there as Area Manager twice nightly many years ago. I was only a young man ... not much money and I stayed in lodgings.

JANE. Oh Reggie ... how funny to imagine you in lodgings. Did you always know you'd get to the top?

WALTER. No my dear. There have been many times when I doubted that very seriously.

JANE. And in your early days in Colwyn Bay, did you ever think that you'd end up with half a column in Who's Who?

WALTER. (*Stops playing.*) Really?

JANE. You must have read it.

WALTER. Someone did show it to me once, when I was staying with the Bedfords at Woburn. (*He resumes playing.*)

JANE. But I suppose being the man you are ... it meant very little?

WALTER. I'm afraid so! All my life I've wanted to stay in the background but people have thrust me to the front.

JANE. What was like at the Palace?

WALTER. Crystal Palace?

JANE. Buckingham Palace. When you went to get your C.B.E. for services to export.

WALTER. Is that Who's Who again?

JANE. Yes.

WALTER. She was very charming.

JANE. I can imagine. And who was the lady who made you an offer when you were a young man?

WALTER. My landlady. Thank God I accepted because I've never had another offer since. Oh dear! Hey ho! Such is life! (*He stops playing at the same point and rises.*) Would you mind *terribly* if I didn't play any more? I feel so frightfully miserable tonight, even my music isn't cheering me up. (*He goes to the window. She goes slowly to the sofa.*)

JANE. You know, Reggie, when I think of all the women who must have offered themselves to you over the years ... offers you were not even aware of, it makes you even more attractive.

WALTER. My dear, it's most awfully, dreadfully, kind of you to try and build up my shattered ego, but the fact remains ... my wife has had a long affair with another man and made me look a complete fool and that is the end of it.

JANE. Come here, Reggie. (*He goes to her slowly ... warily. She takes his hand and draws down him to the sofa.*) Shall we be fools together?

WALTER. I don't quite understand.

JANE. No, you wouldn't. You're so lovely, Reggie! (*She kisses him.*) Shall we console each other for the terrible pain they've given us? After all, they've been doing it for ten days every year for the past three years. If we did it ... just the once ... it would be such poetic justice ... don't you think? (*Pause.*) What do you think about us making love?

WALTER. (*He stretches his mouth.*) Think? At this moment, I haven't a coherent thought in my head.

JANE. But perhaps ... (*She undoes his scarf.*) ... you don't find me attractive? (*She kisses him again.*)

WALTER. My dear Deirdre, I think you are the most devastating, enchanting, beautiful creature I have ever met! I simply, absolutely adore every delectable ounce of you! (*They go into a passionate kiss.*)

JANE. But perhaps you don't feel like it? Perhaps you've got jet lag?

WALTER. I'm not lagging in any department!

JANE. Oh good! (*She rises briskly and takes off her jewelry. Phone rings.*)

WALTER. Ignore it. Can't possibly be for me. (*Phone stops. She begins to undo her dress.*)

JANE. I make only one condition!

WALTER. Yes ... yes ... any condition!

JANE. That you tell Marcia afterwards!

WALTER. I will ... I will!

JANE. I would like that.

WALTER. So would I. You will tell your husband, of course?

JANE. When the right moment arrives. Come on, Reggie ... (*She goes to the door and stops.*) No need to lack confidence with me! I think you're the tastiest man I've met for years. And I've never had such a lovely present before. (*She spreads out her hand to her to herself, then goes into the bedroom.*)

WALTER. (*Rises ... stares blankly ... then goes slowly to the door and stops at the open door.*) You know, Jane ... I do think this is a frightfully good idea of yours. (*Stops in the doorway.*) Oh I say! How spiffing you look just lying there! This morning I never dreamt my day would end like this. (*He enters. Slight pause.*)

JANE. (*Off.*) Oh Reggie!

WALTER. (*Off.*) Oh Jane!

JANE. (*Off.*) Oh Reggie ... that is heaven! (*Pause.*) What could she see in Brian after you, Reggie! Fantastic! Oh Reggie, such bliss! Oh Reggie! Reggie!! Reggie! Oh my God ...!!

WALTER. Oh, Maggie!

JANE. Jane!

(*Lights fade to black then up. MARCIA enters the front door warily.*)

MARCIA. Hello? (*Slight pause. She looks into the study then enters the living room. She sighs*

*with relief as she sees it empty then takes off her
coat and puts it on a chair upstage. Bedroom door
opens and JANE appears and turns back to speak
within.)*

JANE. Bye bye Reggie! It was sheer magic!
(*MARCIA scuttles under the piano. We see her
reaction throughout.)* No stay there darling. You
deserve a little rest. (*JANE goes to her handbag
and puts on some lipstick.)*

WALTER. (*Off.*) No, I must see you off my
darling. (*WALTER appears at the door doing up a
dressing gown.)*

JANE. No really Reggie, I never dreamed you
were going to be as lovely as this!

WALTER. Awfully sweet of you! You're
terribly kind.

JANE. No, I mean it. Brian never made me
feel like this. What can Marcia see in him?
You're so tender ... so sensitive to every nuance of
my body.

WALTER. Terribly nice of you, Jane.

JANE. Then when the moment comes you just
sweep me up, toss me to the ceiling, make me hit
the roof and then make me come apart.

WALTER. Did I do all that?

JANE. And you've been travelling in a plane
for nine hours. What would you be like first thing
in the morning?

WALTER. It was pretty wonderful for me too,
you know.

JANE. You're not just saying that?

WALTER. I can tell you from the bottom of my heart, Jane, that you going to bed with me this evening has been the most astonishing experience of my life!

JANE. I can't believe that!

WALTER. I swear it. If I never work again I swear it. If I spend my remaining days on this earth playing Father Christmas at Harrods I swear it

JANE. Why should you be Father Christmas at Harrods?

WALTER. I meant playing Father Christmas at Harlow New Town. I do it every year for my workers in the factory.

JANE. Oh Reggie! What a beautiful man you are! And was I really more exciting than Marcia?

WALTER. More exciting than Marcia? Don't make me laugh. She just lies there like a log of wood.

JANE. But that's not possible! You're such a sensational lover.

WALTER. Once she even fell asleep.

JANE. (*Shrieks.*) Can't believe it! Not with *you* - Brian, yes.

WALTER. Promise! She dropped off then woke up and said have you started yet? (*They shriek with laughter.*)

JANE. I'm sorry to laugh. How could she? You're divine at it! (*She kisses him then takes his arm and walks him out into the hall.*) So I'll see you next Thursday at my shop? (*MARCIA frozen by this.*)

WALTER. Not half.

JANE. It's my early closing day so be there about one.

WALTER. I'll come as soon as I've signed on.

JANE. Signed on?

WALTER. Signed on my cheques. Thursday is my day for signing the company cheques.

JANE. You know, Reggie, up until today, a multiple orgasm was just something I had read about in Cosmopolitan. Au revoir, my darling. (*Kisses him lightly and goes.*)

WALTER. Au revoir, my darling. (*He closes the door and blinks in a trance-like state, then leaps in the air and dances back into the living room.*) Au revoir, my darling! (*Singing the first line of "I'm Sitting on Top of the World"* he dances to the piano and goes into "My Blue Heaven." MARCIA leaps up from under the piano.*)

MARCIA. How dare you!

WALTER. (*Jumps.*) Oh madam! Where did you come from?

MARCIA. How dare you tell her I'm a log of wood in bed! I never told you to tell her that.

---

* See Music Note, p. 4

WALTER. (*Backs.*) I agree, madam. That wasn't what we rehearsed at all! I'm on your side there ...

MARCIA. I didn't pay you to insult me!

WALTER. I know madam. I was just making conversation.

MARCIA. How dare you humiliate me like that?

WALTER. I had to return her compliments didn't I?

MARCIA. (*Tearfully.*) How could you say I fell asleep during it?

WALTER. I wouldn't have done had I known you were listening, madam.

MARCIA. That wasn't in our agreement!

WALTER. It wasn't! It wasn't! You are right and I am wrong, but after you left she started to undress ... she made all the running ... I had to go along with it didn't I? Keep my end up, conversationally?

MARCIA. I don't object to you making love to her.

WALTER. No?

MARCIA. I like the idea very much. Her going to bed with my decorator thinking it's my husband, amuses me a lot, but you telling her I was boring in bed does not amuse me. Come here, Mr. Page. (*She pulls a chair to the desk.*)

WALTER. (*Nervously.*) I didn't mean to upset you, madam. I didn't even know you were listening ...

you next Thursday at my shop? (*MARCIA frozen by this.*)

WALTER. Not half.

JANE. It's my early closing day so be there about one.

WALTER. I'll come as soon as I've signed on.

JANE. Signed on?

WALTER. Signed on my cheques. Thursday is my day for signing the company cheques.

JANE. You know, Reggie, up until today, a multiple orgasm was just something I had read about in Cosmopolitan. Au revoir, my darling. (*Kisses him lightly and goes.*)

WALTER. Au revoir, my darling. (*He closes the door and blinks in a trance-like state, then leaps in the air and dances back into the living room.*) Au revoir, my darling! (*Singing the first line of "I'm Sitting on Top of the World"* he dances to the piano and goes into "My Blue Heaven." MARCIA leaps up from under the piano.*)

MARCIA. How dare you!

WALTER. (*Jumps.*) Oh madam! Where did you come from?

MARCIA. How dare you tell her I'm a log of wood in bed! I never told you to tell her that.

---

* See Music Note, p. 4

WALTER. (*Backs.*) I agree, madam. That wasn't what we rehearsed at all! I'm on your side there ...

MARCIA. I didn't pay you to insult me!

WALTER. I know madam. I was just making conversation.

MARCIA. How dare you humiliate me like that?

WALTER. I had to return her compliments didn't I?

MARCIA. (*Tearfully.*) How could you say I fell asleep during it?

WALTER. I wouldn't have done had I known you were listening, madam.

MARCIA. That wasn't in our agreement!

WALTER. It wasn't! It wasn't! You are right and I am wrong, but after you left she started to undress ... she made all the running ... I had to go along with it didn't I? Keep my end up, conversationally?

MARCIA. I don't object to you making love to her.

WALTER. No?

MARCIA. I like the idea very much. Her going to bed with my decorator thinking it's my husband, amuses me a lot, but you telling her I was boring in bed does not amuse me. Come here, Mr. Page. (*She pulls a chair to the desk.*)

WALTER. (*Nervously.*) I didn't mean to upset you, madam. I didn't even know you were listening ...

hopeless at it. We all know that! I'm far better. Her husband has been telling me for years.

WALTER. Ah yes ... well that's a different kettle of fish, madam. I mean if I knew that what I was writing was the truth ... fair enough. I could write to her because in that case I wouldn't be lying ... I wouldn't be denying my own feelings.

MARCIA. I see, so at the moment this letter poses a moral problem for you?

WALTER. Yes, it does give me insoluble problems of conduct. (*MARCIA exits into bedroom leaving door ajar.*) I do owe it to you, madam. I admit that. I should write that letter. It's just that I can't at the moment. I'm totally in the wrong. I agree with you ... Mrs. Erskine mustn't be allowed to continue to think you are a log of wood in bed. That's not right at all. She's left here this evening thinking that Reggie is bored with his wife. That's not fair at all. I do see that. I should write that letter. I must rectify the situation. A situation I have caused. It's just that she really was so wonderful. She made me feel so great. I just can't bring myself to lie to her.

MARCIA. (*Comes out of the bedroom in a long black nightdress.*) Would you put the chain on the door please, Mr. Page?

WALTER. (*He goes to it.*) There's only a chain this side.

MARCIA. Yes.

WALTER. If I put it on I can't go home.

MARCIA. You're not going home, Mr. Page.

WALTER. No?

MARCIA. Come in here, Mr. Page. Perhaps we can solve your insoluble problem of conduct. (*She goes into the bedroom leaving the door open.*

WALTER. (*He slowly puts on the chain and enters the living room removing his helmet.*) Really this is most considerate of you, madam. Very kind of you to take the trouble. (*He goes into the bedroom. Shuts the door.*)

CURTAIN

FURNITURE AND PROPERTY LIST

ACT I

<u>Marcia's living room section</u>:

<u>On stage:</u> Sofa with cushions on rubber strap supports; Armchair; Antique cane seated chair; Baby grand piano draped with cloth which conceals a section underneath. On cloth: Pair of vases, Photographs in frames; Small table with bowl; Desk: on it - Telephone, papers, pens, note pad; Sideboard: on it - Bottle of brandy and sherry, Glasses; Bust of Victorian General or similar; Dresden type vase on table near to bedroom; Front door with chain.

<u>Study section:</u> Various items of furniture hidden under decorators' sheets or dust cloths; Electric kettle; Step ladders with plank between bearing tins of paint, brushes, decorators' tools, etc.

<u>Off stage:</u> Motor bike Helmet; Plastic shopping bag containing overalls, lunch box with sandwiches and cassette player. Small cardboard toupee box. (Walter)

Personal: Marcia: Pill box with pills; Walter: Brown socks darned in red; Jane: Handbag containing mallet, pad and pencil.

Front door equipped with chain; Bedroom door capable of being locked off-stage.

Furniture note for Study: Some tall items draped in dust cloths capable of concealing Walter when Jane searches the flat.

ACT II

Marcia's living room section:

On stage: Cushions and bust on cardboard box to approximate height of person playing Jane. Antique type chair with cane seat in prominent position. Note: This chair with seat arranged to give way when trod on by Walter must also be wide enough to accommodate, comfortably, the hips of actress playing Jane. Newspaper.

Study section: Walter's motor cycling gear; Bowler hat; suitcase.

Offstage: Tray with two cups and saucers, milk jug and two pots of tea; plate of Jaffa cakes; plate with sliced lemon.

Personal: Walter: Reggie's suit, tie, shirt and shoes which do not fit; Moustache for his entrance as Reggie. Spectacles in breast pocket of suit; watch; front door key; silk dressing gown and

scarf set for quick change.<u>Marcia:</u> Watch;
whitening lotion for pale complexion effect;
jacket; small case; ruby ring. <u>Jane</u>: Jewelers
eyeglass in handbag; lipstick.

<u>Offstage:</u> Second dressing gown (Walter);
Black night dress. (Marcia); Handbag with purse
and money (Marcia).

EFFECTS PLOT

ACT I

Cue 1	After Marcia exits into bedroom Walter switches on cassette player. Mozart's Horn Concerto music.	Page 12
Cue 2	Walter opens a tin of paint. Door bell.	Page 13
Cue 3	Walter turns off cassette. Stop music.	Page 13
Cue 4	Walter rinses paint brush. Telephone rings.	Page 25
Cue 5	Walter scratches Marcia. Telephone rings.	Page 30
Cue 6	Walter shoots his cuffs. Sound of tearing cloth.	Page 55
Cue 7	Walter's foot goes through seat. Sound of wood and cane splintering. Door bell.	Page 63

Cue 8	Marcia sits at piano and plays Clementine. Piano music.	Page 74
Cue 9	Walter sits at piano and plays opening bars of "I'll See you Again." Piano music.	Page 89
Cue 10	Walter stops playing. End piano music.	Page 89
Cue 11	Walter resumes playing. Start piano music	Page 90
Cue 12	Walter stops playing. End piano music.	Page 90
Cue 13	Walter starts song again. Piano music resumes and continues.	Page 90
Cue 14	Walter stops playing. Stop piano music.	Page 91
Cue 15	Walter resumes playing. Resume piano music	Page 93
Cue 16	Walter finally stops playing. End piano music.	Page 94
Cue 17	Jane takes off jewelry. Telephone rings.	Page 95
Cue 18	Walter sings. Piano music of "My Blue Heaven".	Page 99

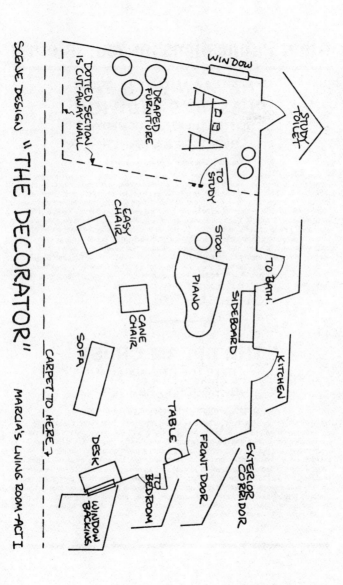

SCENE DESIGN "THE DECORATOR" MARCIA'S LIVING ROOM-ACT I

WINDOW

STUDY TOILET

DRAPED FURNITURE

DOTTED SECTION IS CUT-AWAY WALL

TO STUDY

EASY CHAIR

STOOL

PIANO

TO BATH.

SIDEBOARD

CANE CHAIR

KITCHEN

SOFA

TABLE

FRONT DOOR

EXTERIOR CORRIDOR

DESK

TO BEDROOM

WINDOW BACKING

CARPET TO HERE ↑

Other Publications for Your Interest

THE MAN WITH THE PLASTIC SANDWICH

(LITTLE THEATRE—COMEDY)

By ROGER KARSHNER

2 men, 2 women—Simple exterior

Walter Price, a "basic blue" individual, is thrown out of work after twenty years with the same firm. During an anxiety-laden period of job hunting and readjustment Walter attempts to find solace on a bench in an urban park. Here he is confronted by three engaging, provocative characters. First there is Ellie, a high-spirited ingenue who represents hope; then Haley, a distinguished hobo representing wisdom; and finally Lenore, a hooker who represents reality. Each encounter enlightens Walter, gives him perspective, and ultimately new purpose and direction. A very funny play with bittersweet moments and three dimensional characters. "You will laugh until your sides feel as if they will burst, until your eyes begin to water, until you are sure that one more clever line or witty exchange will send you into a laughing fit from which you may never recover."—Chicago Sun-Times. "This play is truly high comedy and I can't think of a soul who wouldn't love the off-beat characters portrayed in this 4-spoked comedic wheel."—Chicago Reporter/Progress Newspapers.

THE DREAM CRUST

(LITTLE THEATRE—DRAMA)

By ROGER KARSHNER

3 men, 3 women, 1 10-year-old boy —Interior

Named in the Bruns-Mantle Yearbook as one of America's Best Plays. Frank Haynes, an earth-loving farmer, has given up his hound-dogging and high times under the pressure of the family's admonition that "A man has got to get ahead." Haynes would be happy to do nothing but tend his farm and reap whatever profit it might generate. But he realizes that there are five mouths depending on him and the lure of big money available to him in a nearby big-city factory too great to ignore. Set against a backdrop of the land-locked Midwest, the play dramatizes a man's persistent, agonizing search for personal freedom and the sense of loss between father and son. "A moving portrait of a land-locked family that needs to be seen."—Variety. "The plays' spirit, its underlying warmth, particularly in the unspoken father-son relationship, creates a world that's identifiable and that breathes."—L.A. Herald-Examiner.

Other Publications for Your Interest

GROWN UPS
(LITTLE THEATRE—COMEDY)
By JULES FEIFFER

2 men, 3 women, 1 female child—Interiors

An acerbic comedy by the famed cartoonist and author of *Knock Knock* and *Little Murders*. It's about a middle-aged journalist who has, at last, grown-up—only to find he's trapped in a world of emotional infants. "A laceratingly funny play about the strangest of human syndromes—the love that kills rather than comforts. Feiffer's vision seems merciless, but its mercy is the fierce comic clarity with which he exposes every conceivable permutation of smooth-tongued cruelty . . . Feiffer constructs a fiendishly complex machine of reciprocal irritation in which Jake (the journalist), his parents, his wife and his sister carp, cavil, harass, hector and finally attack one another with relentless trivia that detonate deeply buried resentments like emotional land mines . . . Moving past Broadway one-liners and easy gags, (Feiffer) makes laughter an adventure . . . This farce is Feiffer's exclusive specialty, and it's never been more harrowingly hilarious."—Newsweek. "Savagely funny."—N.Y. Times. "A compelling, devastating evening of theatre . . . the first adult play of the season."—Women's Wear Daily.   (#9125)

LUNCH HOUR
(LITTLE THEATRE—COMEDY)
By JEAN KERR

3 men, 2 women—Interior

Never has Jean Kerr's wit had a keener edge or her comic sense more peaks of merriment than in this clever confection, starring Gilda Radner and Sam Waterston as a pair whose spouses are having an affair, and who have to counter by inventing an affair of their own. He, ironically, is a marriage counsellor, and a bit of a stick. His wife juggles husband, lover and mother and is a real go-getter. In fact, it was she who proposed to him. Of the other couple, the wife is a bit kooky. She can discourse on things tacky while wearing an evening gown with her jogging sneakers on; or, again, be overjoyed at the prospect of a trip to Paris: "And we'll never have to ask for french fried potatoes. They'll just come like that." While her husband, "Well, he's rich for a living." Or as he expresses it: "It's very difficult to do something if you don't need any money." All ends forgivingly for both couples, as the aggrieved wife concedes that they both "need something to regret," and the other husband concedes "I knew when I married that everyone would want to dance with you." "Civilized, charming, stylish . . . Very warm and most amusing . . . delicately interweaves laughter and romance."—N.Y. Times. "An amiable comedy about the eternal quadrangle . . . The author's most entertaining play in years."—N.Y. Daily News. "A beautiful weave of plot, character and laughs . . . It's delicious."—NBC-TV.   (#674)

Other Publications for Your Interest

NOISES OFF
(LITTLE THEATRE—FARCE)

By MICHAEL FRAYN

5 men, 4 women—2 Interiors

This wonderful Broadway smash hit is "a farce about farce, taking the clichés of the genre and shaking them inventively through a series of kaleidoscopic patterns. Never missing a trick, it has as its first act a pastiche of traditional farce; as its second, a contemporary variant on the formula; as its third, an elaborate undermining of it. The play opens with a touring company dress-rehearsing 'Nothing On', a conventional farce. Mixing mockery and homage, Frayn heaps into this play-within-a-play a hilarious melee of stock characters and situations. Caricatures—cheery char, outraged wife and squeaky blonde—stampede in and out of doors. Voices rise and trousers fall . . . a farce that makes you think as well as laugh."—London Times Literary Supplement. ". . . as side-splitting a farce as I have seen. Ever? *Ever.*"—John Simon, NY Magazine. "The term 'hilarious' must have been coined in the expectation that something on the order of this farce-within-a-farce would eventually come along to justify it."—N.Y. Daily News. "Pure fun."—N.Y. Post. "A joyous and loving reminder that the theatre really does go on, even when the show falls apart."—N.Y. Times.   (#16052)

THE REAL THING
(ADVANCED GROUPS—COMEDY)

By TOM STOPPARD

4 men, 3 women—Various settings

The effervescent Mr. Stoppard has never been more intellectually—and *emotionally*—engaging than in this "backstage" comedy about a famous playwright named Henry Boot whose second wife, played on Broadway to great acclaim by Glenn Close (who won the Tony Award), is trying to merge "worthy causes" (generally a euphemism for left-wing politics) with her art as an actress. She has met a "political prisoner" named Brodie who has been jailed for radical thuggery, and who has written an inept play about how property is theft, about how the State stifles the Rights of The Individual, etc., etc., etc. Henry's wife wants him to make the play work theatrically, which he does after much soul-searching. Eventually, though, he is able to convince his wife that Brodie is emphatically *not* a victim of political repression. He is, in fact, a *thug*. Famed British actor Jeremy Irons triumphed in the Broadway production (Tony Award), which was directed to perfection by none other than Mike Nichols (Tony Award). "So densely and entertainingly packed with wit, ideas and feelings that one visit just won't do . . . Tom Stoppard's most moving play and the most bracing play anyone has written about love and marriage in years."—N.Y. Times. "Shimmering, dazzling theatre, a play of uncommon wit and intelligence which not only thoroughly delights but challenges and illuminates our lives."—WCBS-TV. 1984 Tony Award-Best Play.   (#941)